Compensation Plans for Law Firms

Second Edition

Edited by James D. Cotterman

Altman Weil Pensa, Inc.

The Section of Law Practice Management, American Bar Association, offers an educational program for lawyers in practice. Books and other materials are published in furtherance of that program. Authors and editors of publications may express their own legal interpretations and opinions, which are not necessarily those of either the American Bar Association or the Section of Law Practice Management unless adopted pursuant to the By-laws of the Association. The opinions expressed do not reflect in any way a position of the Section or the American Bar Association.

Printed in the United States of America.

Library of Congress Catalog Card Number 95-79031
ISBN 1-57073-192-6

00 99 98 97 96   5 4 3 2 1

Discounts are available for books ordered in bulk. Special consideration is given to state bars, CLE programs, and other bar-related organizations. Inquire at Publications Planning & Marketing, American Bar Association, 750 N. Lake Shore Drive, Chicago, Illinois 60611.

Contents

Foreword

When Altman & Weil's *Compensation Plans for Lawyers and Their Staffs* was released in 1986, it quickly proved to be a useful tool for law firms seeking to develop equitable ways of distributing profit to the owners of the legal business, and to pay employees for their services. Law firms throughout the United States read and followed the advice to reward the variable contributions of lawyers in the firm and to implement compensation plans *before* disputes arose over the value of individual contributions to the firm.

Compensation Plans was written by the national legal consulting firm Altman Weil Pensa, including the lead author James D. Cotterman. Altman Weil Pensa was able to bring to the project twenty-five years of experience with law firms of every size. AWP also relied upon data collected annually in the firm's annual survey of law firm compensation.

The decision to produce a new edition of the book reflects both a recognition that changes in law firm economics and management since 1986 have altered many traditional concepts in law firm compensation, and that the first edition did not address compensation of nonpartners in as much depth as the subject deserved. Accordingly, the Second Edition brings to the table concepts that have undergone evolution during the past decade, such as value billing, tiered ownership, and deferred compensation. The new edition also provides guidance on how to establish workable plans for compensating associates and other employed lawyers, legal assistants, and professional and clerical staff. Since all these groups have unique compensation issues, they are discussed separately in the book.

Because quality in law practice is correlated to maintaining stability in both the partnership ranks and staff, and because stability is related to satisfaction, and a significant factor in satisfaction is the element of monetary reward for services rendered, it follows that compensation is a major key to quality practice. A firm that attracts good people, pays them what they are worth, provides incentives for growth, and communicates fairness in its compensation decisions is more likely to generate loyalty and commitment to the firm than organizations lacking such an environment.

The concepts articulated in this book are important for firms of all sizes, although certain ideas may prove more viable in small firms, large firms, or solo practices. There is no magic formula that will work for all firms, but with this resource, law firm leaders can craft a compensation plan that meets their own unique needs and circumstances.

Professor Gary A. Munneke
Chair, LPM Publishing

Acknowledgments

This manuscript was based on that prepared by Altman & Weil, Inc., and published by the American Bar Association Law Practice Management Section in 1986. It has been revised substantially and expanded by James Cotterman, assisted by Ward Bower, Thomas Clay, and Peter Giuliani. Thanks to Diane Quinn and Michele Dowd for the transcription and proofreading of the text.

About Altman Weil Pensa, Inc.

Altman Weil Pensa, Inc., is a management consulting firm specializing in providing a wide range of services to legal organizations throughout the world. Founded in 1970, its headquarters are in suburban Philadelphia (Newtown Square, Pennsylvania), with offices in Connecticut, North Carolina, Wisconsin, and Washington State.

Altman Weil Pensa professional consulting services include strategic planning, marketing, organizational development, compensation systems, law firm mergers and acquisitions, quality management programs, process reengineering, space planning, recruiting, profitability studies, and technology.

Altman Weil Pensa consultants are authors of major treatises in the legal consulting field, including *How to Manage Your Law Office*, *Law Office Automation and Technology*, and *Introduction to Law Practice Management*, all of which are published by Matthew Bender & Co., Inc., New York. Its consultants have written monographs on lawyer compensation and strategic planning for the American Bar Association's Law Practice Management Section and other major legal and business publications. In addition, Altman Weil Pensa publishes a monthly newsletter, *The Report to Legal Management*.

Since the early 70s, Altman Weil Pensa has published annual surveys on law firm economics, law department salaries, bar counsel salaries, functions and expenditures of corporate law departments, retirement and withdrawal practices of law firms, salaries of corporate patent counsel, compensation systems in private law firms, managing partner and administrator duties and compensation, alternative pricing of legal services and alternative dispute resolution, and law library policies budgets and compensation.

ALTMAN WEIL PENSA, INC.
Two Campus Blvd., Suite 200
Newtown Square, PA 19073
610-359-9900

About the Editor

James D. Cotterman is a senior management consultant with Altman Weil Pensa, Inc., specializing in compensation systems, capitalization, buy-in/buy-out, retirement, profitability analysis, economic forecasting models, turnarounds, mergers, firm documentation, governance, and organizational issues.

Before joining Altman Weil Pensa in 1988, Mr. Cotterman was manager of acquisitions for a public company in the health care industry, where he specialized in the development, analysis, evaluation, and negotiation of mergers.

Mr. Cotterman is a regular contributor to *The Altman Weil Pensa Report to Legal Management,* is on the Board of Editors of *Accounting for Law Firms,* and is the supervising author for *How to Manage Your Law Office.* His writings have appeared in *The American Lawyer, The National Law Journal, ALA Legal Management, Legal Economics, International Law Firm Management, The Practical Lawyer,* and state and local bar publications. Mr. Cotterman has lectured on law firm economics, valuation, retirement, alternative pricing and billing arrangements, collection practices, and capitalization/debt management, including presentations for state and local bar associations and the Association of Legal Administrators Annual Convention Conference.

Academic credentials include an undergraduate degree in Operations Management (1978) and an M.B.A. in Accounting (1983), both from Syracuse University. Mr. Cotterman is a licensed Certified Public Accountant in the Commonwealth of Pennsylvania (1985), and is a member of the American and Pennsylvania Institutes of Certified Public Accountants.

Introduction

Compensation. Mention this word in almost any work setting and blood pressures rise, pulse rates quicken, defensive mechanisms ready. Why? We all work for money. Compensation represents a tangible expression of a person's value. It defines lifestyle, position within a community, status among peers, friends, and family, and it measures the relative importance of the individual to the organization. Compensation is one of the most complex and emotional issues that confront any business enterprise. Economics, psychology, sociology, politics, and ethics are all components in the compensation transaction.

Each individual makes a personal judgment about the appropriateness (read fairness) of his or her compensation in two ways. First is the direct comparison to coworkers' compensation. In this instance, a large variation is often better accepted than a small difference. Second is the perceived economic comparison with others in the community. This is an analysis of lifestyle (home, cars, activities, and the like). Issues of fairness do more to disrupt business objectives, cause employees to change jobs, or make us feel pleasure or despair than almost any other.

The predominant reason free agency took hold of the legal profession was compensation. The legal market is extremely competitive and MR-5.6 (formerly DR2-108) effectively allows partners and shareholders in law firms to change firms and take their clients with them whenever they choose to do so. As a result, partners or shareholders with a book of business that would entitle them to greater compensation elsewhere frequently leave their firms. The result is that frequently the most productive partners or shareholders defect—along with their revenue streams—placing a firm in severe jeopardy.

Make no mistake about the importance of compensation. Seventy-five percent of every fee dollar goes toward compensation in a law firm, be it associate and support staff salary and benefits or partner incomes. It represents, in the aggregate, the largest and most significant set of transactions a law firm makes. Failure to attend properly to compensation issues can have disastrous consequences, including low productivity, high turnover, client dissatisfaction, low employee morale, and disputes with former partners and former and existing employees.

Law firms are closely held businesses with active owner participation in their affairs. As such, any treatise on compensation for law firms must distinguish compensation systems for the active owners from compensation systems for the nonowner employees. Owner compensation is as much a political transaction as it is an exchange for services. Compensation for nonowners does not typically involve the political element. While there are many similarities, owner compensation issues are fundamentally more difficult.

This book is divided into five chapters that discuss the following topics:

1. Partner/Shareholder compensation,
2. "Of counsel" compensation,
3. Associate compensation,
4. Paraprofessional compensation, and
5. Staff compensation.

COMPENSATION THEORY

Before we begin to examine compensation plans, let's discuss compensation theory. Central to this topic is the concept of a labor market. A labor market is the geographic area from which a business is likely to employ workers. It also defines the area within which it must establish its competitive position to attract and retain the caliber of worker desired. For example, the hourly support staff (secretaries, receptionists, bookkeepers, clerks, and the like) are drawn from a very local market. They are unlikely to travel outside a well defined and limited area to seek employment. Lawyers, however, are quite mobile and can easily qualify to work in many jurisdictions. They represent a national labor market. It is likely that a law firm across the nation could compete for a lawyer in your community.

Early in a lawyer's career, academic credentials significantly impact the graduate's effective labor market. The reputation and prestige of the schools attended and the level of academic excellence achieved are defining factors. Graduates from national schools generally have opportunities anywhere in the country. Graduates from state or regional schools may need to confine their search to that geographic region where their school is known. Finally, graduates from local institutions, such as an evening law school, are likely to be limited in their opportunities to the city or state within which the school is located.

As a lawyer becomes admitted in one or more jurisdictions, gains experience, and specializes either in an area of the law, an industry, or a geographic market for clients (e.g., Asia), the labor market available to him or her changes. The market may be industry-related. The tax laws for insurance companies are unlike the tax laws pertaining to almost all other companies. Consequently, the labor market for insurance tax lawyers is different from the labor market for corporate tax lawyers in general. The market may also cut across industries and relate to a practice area or practice segment. Patent lawyers tend to have a technical specialty. The market for a patent lawyer with an organic chemistry background is likely to be different from the market for a patent lawyer with an electrical engineering background. The market for international lawyers with an Asian focus is likely to be different from that of lawyers with a Latin American or European focus.

Development of a client base may inhibit geographic opportunities for lawyers as they mature in their profession. If a client base is national, the potential labor market and relocation opportunities may not be limited to any great extent. However, if the client base is regional or confined to a single state or limited to a community, the labor market is much narrower and opportunities to relocate without significant negative economic impact are more limited.

Understanding the labor market in which a firm competes for talent, as well as the appropriate skill levels required, are central in making compensation decisions. If a firm competes in the national labor market, it must understand national compensation patterns. If it hires from a local market, national standards are less important; the firm must consider the prevailing local conditions.

Labor markets are rarely easily defined, discrete entities. They overlap. The various market-defining components of a position may operate in different labor markets. This concept could be illustrated with the Olympic symbol of interlocking rings.

If there is a universal rule with respect to compensation, it is this: Every compensation system works—every compensation system fails. Systems can run the spectrum from objective to subjective, participative to dictatorial. What works in any particular law firm is a system that fits the culture and personalities of the partners. That means that a good compensation system should be flexible; it should be able to survive evolving needs of the firm as well as changing ownership. A system must be embraced by the partners and be consistent with their collective philosophy, background, and perspective.

Despite their differences, all successful compensation systems feature two common qualities. These qualities are inextricably linked to each other, ideally forming a bond that stands the test of time.

First and foremost, a successful system must be fair and be perceived as fair by the partners who are essential to the firm's economic success and reputation. The perception of fairness is critical. Even a system that is fair in objective reality cannot survive if a substantial number of the key players perceive it to be unfair. Fairness should not be confused with satisfaction with one's own compensation. Fairness is measured by a sense of equity in treatment with respect to others and by others. To determine the fairness of a compensation system, partners may want to ask themselves some important questions:

- Do I understand the system?
- Does the system recognize what individuals contribute to the organization?

- Are the rules clear?
- Are the rules followed and applied in a consistent manner from person to person and from year to year?
- Are the compensators individuals who are trusted and respected?

These questions define the perception of fairness. Inherent in such questions is a determination of the fairness perceived from relative levels of compensation internally and externally.

A second quality of successful compensation systems is that of simplicity. Altman Weil Pensa's experience has shown that there is a direct correlation between the simplicity of a compensation system and the degree to which wage earners understand how their compensation is determined. That, in turn, goes a long way toward the perception of fairness. Simplicity is the foundation. Each additional consideration or step in a compensation system should be measured against simplicity. One might ask:

- Are we truly gaining an insight into an individual's contribution that is worth the additional complexity?

COMPENSATION PLANS AND THE LAW FIRM

The difficulty in structuring a compensation system for a law firm is in selecting the best mix of compensable criteria and the right amount of participation that is consistent with the firm's needs and its culture. A law firm is fluid through time. Because of these changes, the compensation system needs to function like a good constitution—grounded in good basic principles and subject to amendment only after careful, thoughtful deliberation. The experience and objectivity of an expert outsider and the candor of confidential input often work together to evolve a firm's compensation system.

An important event in any law firm is the exchange of individual expectations with respect to compensation.

- What are our objectives? Formal or informal?
- How much money is enough?
- How much money is not enough?
- What does compensation mean, both personally and professionally, to each individual?
- What level of risk sharing should take place?
- How much disparity should exist from top to bottom?

These questions define much about how economic rewards can be fashioned and how they are divided among lawyers. They may even lead to a conclusion that there are partners who can no longer be members of the firm, or associates who should no longer be employed.

There is an additional factor significant to compensation in law firms. The legal profession is maturing. As such, the balance is shifting from the supplier (lawyers) to the consumer (clients). The profession experienced an explosion in the number of lawyers, paralegals, and support personnel during the 1970s and 1980s. Positions that never existed in 1960 now have their own trade associations—for example, legal administrators (ALA), legal assistants (NALA), and marketing directors (NALFMA). Management Information Systems (MIS) directors now preside over the proliferation of technology throughout law firms.

Concurrent with the growth in the numbers of personnel was an explosion in the starting salaries of new graduates. Nationally, new graduates' starting salaries rose from a median of $14,000 in 1973 to a peak of $50,000 in 1989.[1] That represents an increase of 257 percent as compared to a 184 percent increase in the consumer price index (CPI) for the same period. Fortunately, law firms have held the line on offers to recent graduates to a national median of $50,000 for the past five years.[2] According to another study, the national median salary for the graduating class of 1993 was $48,000 for the 59 percent of the 15,214 graduates who entered private practice and reported such information.[3] That's up from $47,500 for the 64 percent of the 14,190 graduates who entered private practice from the class of 1992 and reported such information.

Along with exploding salaries came the new expenses associated with the automated law office. Law firms invested in technology—at first in the accounting department and in word processing, then in secretarial and paralegal workstations, and now for lawyers. Power typewriters were replaced with word processors, which were replaced with stand-alone computers, which were replaced with integrated networks. Phone systems, copiers, fax machines, data lines, fax modems, image scanners, and automated cost tracking devices all required investment dollars. Technology enhancements came so quickly that by the 1990s one could be assured that the latest technology today would be obsolete within six months.

Unfortunately, the growth in fee volume of legal work has not kept pace with the growth in suppliers of legal services. Couple this with aggressive pressure by management to drive nonproductive costs out of their organizations, and the result is a legal market where vast changes are taking place in the profitability of legal services and the means of delivering legal services. The impact has been keenly felt with law firm dissolutions, stagnant (or declining) lawyer compensation, lack of employment, and lower margins on services rendered.

Figure I.1 illustrates the change in relationships of compensation as compared to an index of recent graduate starting levels of compensation. This illustration sets median starting salaries of recent graduates at a constant value of 100 and relates the median earnings of other groups to it. Comparisons are made for third-year associates, partners with nine years of experience, partners with between twenty-five and twenty-nine years of experience, and all partners as a group. In 1977, an experienced partner earned 4.9 times more than a new associate. Twelve years later, that relationship hit a low of 3.6. It has risen marginally since. Of all groups examined, only three-year associates ended at a higher multiple than in 1977, primarily due to the 1989 peak in starting salary offers to recent graduates.

FIG. I.1 **Relative Median Compensation of Lawyers in Private Practice**

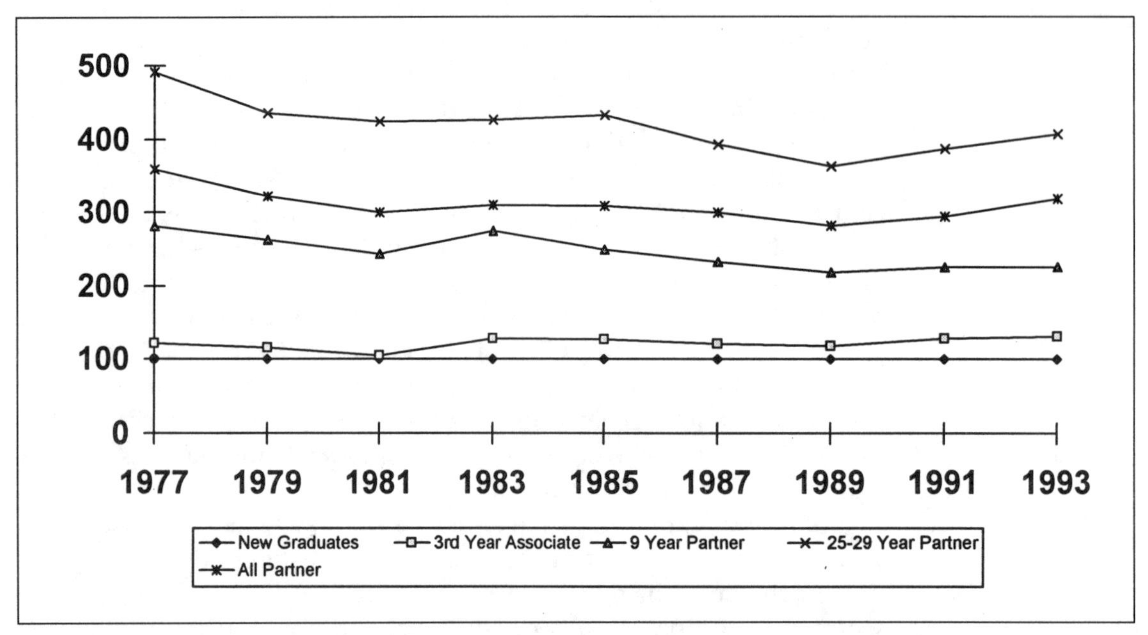

Source: *1994 Survey of Law Firm Economics*. Altman Weil Pensa Publications, Inc., Newtown Square, PA 19073

Law has become a very competitive profession. That coupled with a new economy, significant likelihood of legislative reform, and wary clients, has changed the economics of law practice. Lawyers commonly grapple with the problem of dividing a pie that is not sufficient to satisfy everyone. When dollars are plentiful, many problems are ignored. But, when dollars are tight, internal and external equity becomes increasingly difficult to achieve.

Many of the problems in compensation systems, particularly owner compensation systems, relate not to the matter of income allocation, but to the overall economics of the practice. Often the compensation system is blamed when individual compensation is perceived as inadequate. But, with labor such a significant component of law firm overhead, firm profitability directly affects each worker's compensation. In dealing with problems in compensation systems, attention must be directed to the overall economics of a law firm's performance, as well as to the manner of income allocation.

Law firm owners must allocate limited resources among all of the wage earners. As a consequence, there are no easy compensation answers and complete satisfaction is rarely possible. Instead, partners should strive to reach certain objectives. The basic purposes of any compensation system are to attract and retain talented people, and to stimulate them to pursue activities that contribute to the organization.

PAYROLL CYCLES

The payroll cycle should be regular, balancing the needs of the law firm for efficient administration and the workers' needs for continuing cash flow. Payroll cycles can be paid weekly, bi-weekly (every other week; twenty-six times per year), semi-monthly (twice a month; twenty-four times per year), or monthly. Some firms have alternating payrolls to even out cash flow. An example is alternating bi-weekly payrolls with all staff and associates on one cycle and partners on the other. This works to smooth out cash flow, but it adds to the bookkeeping burdens of the firm. This is true even if the firm uses an outside service for payroll processing, as most firms do.

Generally, support staff, who are lower paid and tend to live from paycheck to paycheck, prefer a weekly or bi-weekly cycle. Semi-monthly and monthly cycles have occasional extra weekends that slip into the pay period, just as employers have two or four months during the year in which an extra paycheck falls. It is more of a hardship for lower-income employees to plan for such occurrences than it is for the firm to plan for its extra cycles. Generally, most firms use a semi-monthly or monthly cycle for owners and either a bi-weekly or semi-monthly cycle for everyone else.

SURVEY DATA

In 1993, Altman Weil Pensa, Inc., conducted a study of law firm compensation systems. Survey data was requested from mailings to readers of Altman Weil Pensa's *Report to Legal Management* and to a select group of law firms that have had contact with Altman Weil Pensa, Inc., through its surveys and consulting services. There were 412 carefully edited responses tabulated. Responses to the compensation systems survey varied most by size of firm. However, certain structural differences between professional corporations and partnerships modified answers to some questions. These differences lie primarily in the tax treatment the organizations and their owners receive.

Summary information from that study (*Compensation Systems in Private Law Firms*) is used throughout this book, as is summary information taken from our annual *Surveys of Law Firm Economics*, our *Managing Partners' Survey*, and our survey on *Retirement and Withdrawal*.

NOTES

1. *Survey of Law Firm Economics* (Newtown Square, PA: Altman Weil Pensa Publications, Inc., 1994).
2. *Id.*
3. *Employment Report and Salary Survey* (Washington, DC: National Association for Law Placement, 1994).

CHAPTER 1

Partner and Shareholder Compensation

OVERVIEW

The form of organization selected by a law firm has significant impact on the tax consequences of its compensation system. It is largely irrelevant, however, as to the principles used to determine compensation within a law firm. For the purpose of our discussion, *salary* and *draw* will be interchangeable terms, as will *bonus* and *distribution*. Documentation differences are very important because of the need to ensure the desired tax consequence of these transactions. Differences in compensation methodology between partnerships and professional corporations are, therefore, primarily driven by the tax treatments the firms and their owners receive.

Devising a compensation program for the owners is, by far, the most difficult compensation-related task. Owners must deal from "inside the circle" on this issue. Associates, of counsel, and staff are all external groups and generally do not have risk-associated attributes in their compensation. It is the compensation for risks taken, the division of profits, the confusion over the separation of the "arms-length" value for an owner's labor, and the division of profits earned by the enterprise in general that create such controversy. This is an issue peculiar to a closely held business, where the owners are active in its day-to-day affairs. In a manufacturing setting, there is much guidance as to the relationships between the value for work rendered and the return on ownership. However, in a law firm there is no such guidance. In fact, the final arbiter in such issues, the Internal Revenue Service, has not been successful in asserting excess compensation claims against professionals operating in a corporate form of organization. Legally, there is no dividing line between profits and the wage earners' efforts in a law firm.

PARTNER AND SHAREHOLDER COMPENSATION CRITERIA

The following unranked attributes regarding law firm owner compensation criteria should assist each reader in positioning his or her own experiences. If your firm is not consistent with the generalities and the system is working, then do nothing. If the system is not working, look for differences and see if they may offer some direction.

Ownership

Partners or shareholders, as owners of an enterprise, are entitled to some reward for their investment and risk. The owners of a law firm are, after all, entrepreneurs. They meet a payroll, accept liability for the firm's activities, and provide capital. The most important asset of a law firm, however, is its clients, and clients cannot be owned or sold. The courts have consistently upheld the client's ultimate right to choose legal representation as a matter of public interest and policy. However, it is possible for a practice to be transferred for consideration. The American Bar Association (ABA) and certain states have set forth guidelines involving such transactions that go beyond the scope of this text. There is, therefore, a very practical limit to the value of ownership.

Some law firms pay interest on capital invested in the firm as a way to reward ownership or to provide a return appropriate to the level of capital invested. In professional corporations, owner capital can be structured as a combination of equity and debt such that a return (interest) is paid on the debt. Although dividends can be declared and paid on equity, it is not tax efficient to do so.

Law firms have moved to separate compensation from ownership. That is, relative compensation levels do not impact or track relative levels of ownership. This should always be true for those lawyers practicing in a professional corporation, to avoid treatment of compensation as dividends, subjecting all or part of it to double taxation. Partnerships over the past half decade have begun to follow. In so doing, the meaning of ownership has changed. Ownership is now looked upon as a means to apportion the owner capital needs of the organization and to establish certain voting rights in the management of the firm's affairs. The level of importance accorded ownership in compensation is rapidly decreasing.

Seniority

Although some firms are entirely structured around length of service in the profession and in the firm, this factor has declined in importance for most law firms in compensation decisions. This came about primarily because of the increasing financial pressures placed on law firms.

However, a key aspect of the strength of any organization is its heritage and stability. Some law firms have sought to preserve or regain these characteristics. Therefore, tenure with the firm is accorded some importance in those firms. These features are gaining increasing importance not only to clients who quickly tire of following their lawyer from firm to firm, but also to lenders and landlords who recognize the importance of those traits in securing the repayment of long-term obligations.

Although years of experience as a practicing lawyer was the least considered factor in owner compensation by respondents in the Altman Weil Pensa, Inc., compensation systems study, there remains a strong correlation between years of experience and compensation that is driven in part by economics (higher billing rates and greater efficiency of experienced fee producers) and by traditional notions of progressive compensation over a career. Illustration 1.1 depicts the general trend of compensation throughout a lawyer's career. Statistically, lawyers' earnings peak between their twenty-fifth and thirtieth year of practice.

Seniority encompasses more than just a person's age or the number of years he or she has spent at a firm. One New England partnership broadly defined seniority to include the "number of years the partner has spent developing and maintaining clients, building and enhancing the firm's reputation, and participating in the training and development of a cadre of lawyers who produce for the benefit of all the partners in the firm."

ILL. 1.1 **Total Compensation—Partners/Shareholders (By years since admission, all firms 1993)**

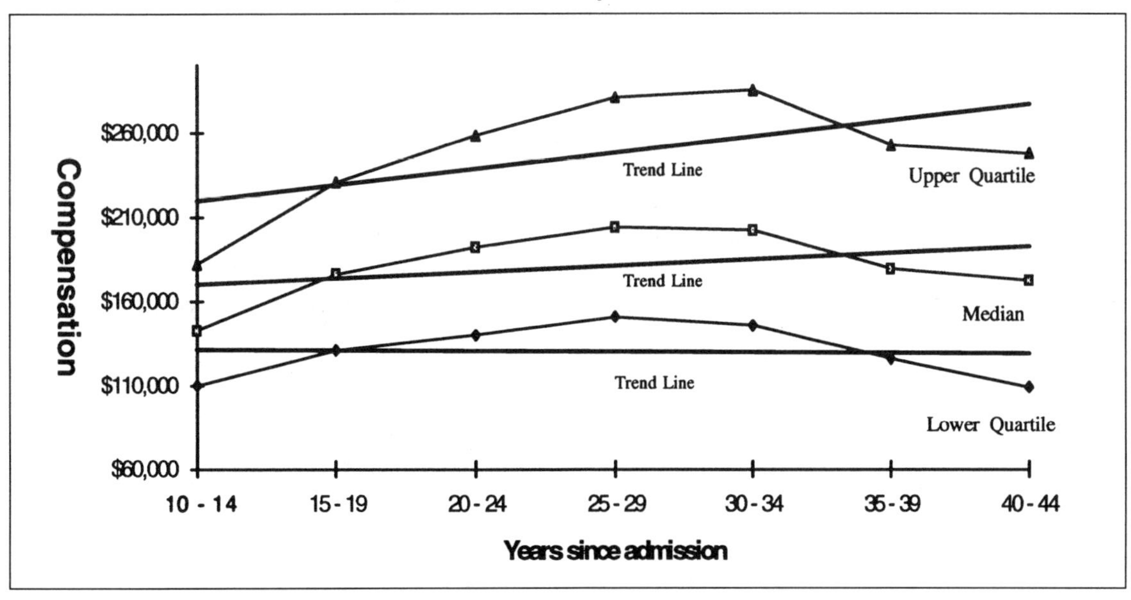

Source: *1994 Survey of Law Firm Economics*. Altman Weil Pensa Publications, Inc., Newtown Square, PA 19073

Pro Bono

Pro bono and other similar nonbillable activities generally are of little importance in compensation. Such endeavors did not translate into fee receipts within the very short-term orientation many partners have with respect to profitability.

Provided the efforts are not overdone and that the activities are coordinated and approved by the firm, they may be considered when compensation is determined.

Teaching, Writing, Speaking

Often lawyers give back to their profession by assisting in the educational process of other lawyers. They may teach continuing legal education classes or lecture at a law school. They may write for legal journals or speak at bar meetings. Aside from the obvious benefit of enhancing the knowledge level of the profession, such individuals establish their own credentials as experts in selected areas of the law. Some firms will choose to reward this activity.

Collegiality/Team Play

Collegiality is adherence to the spirit, as well as the letter, of firm policies, the willingness to "pitch in" when needed, the sense of working and getting along together in a spirit of cooperation, the mutual respect for others' skills, and tolerance for others' weaknesses. It is important to those firms seeking to foster a team orientation. Practicing law is stressful enough—the firm does not need the added stress of "Lone Rangers" (i.e., inconsiderate tyrants or abusive egotists). Creating internal harmony—that is, a sense that the firm will pull together to meet the challenges and demands facing it—is gaining in importance in compensation decisions.

Training

Law firms are in an ongoing process of inducting new members (lawyers, paralegals, and staff) into the organization and integrating them into the work system. In team-oriented firms, such integration is essential and valued accordingly. Because a law firm makes a substantial investment in finding and paying a young lawyer or a novice secretary, and because the quality of supervision, training, and monitoring that inexperienced individuals receive is of significant importance to their development and the quality of service provided to clients, a law firm must be prepared to pay the trainers.

Expertise

Expertise in a specialty or in some facet of professional activity can add to an individual's value as a partner. If a law firm needs the services of a specialist to advertise itself as qualified to its clients, the capabilities of that individual may offset any lack of fee receipts or direct client development.

Legal expertise is most broadly defined as the quality and timeliness of work product and advice, particularly if the expertise is outstanding and the lawyer serves as a resource for others within the firm and legal community. Someone once said they could not define quality, but they could identify unacceptable work product, service, or advice. The following definition, however, used by a client of the author, is particularly appropriate: "Quality includes knowledge of applicable law, imagination, creativity and innovation, ability to write clearly and persuasively, ability to analyze quickly and accurately, good judgment, ability to plan and implement legal strategies, good oral communication skills, the ability to handle the unexpected, the ability to negotiate, and the ability to handle complex matters."

Leadership/Management

In industrial and business settings, management is paid more highly than production, and often more highly than sales, though not necessarily so. In many law firms, management is not paid for at all. Illustration 1.2 provides relative earnings of the highest paid partner, average partner, and lowest paid partner in comparison to managing partner earnings. Generally, if a law firm does not pay for management, it will have little, because free work is grudgingly given. Firm-approved budgets, combined with documented duties and authority, provide a framework for compensation considerations to be granted.

Firm management (defined as the contribution to firm or practice management, including such services as acting as the firm's managing partner, serving on committees, chairing a practice department, recruiting and training professional employees, and the like) is a necessary and important function in any modern law firm. Good management requires time and effort[1]—the same time and effort one would otherwise devote to fee-paying clients. Recognition by the firm of the importance of management and the sacrifices made by good managers are crucial.

As firms grow, management functions become more centralized. This is necessary to carry out the functions of the firm in an orderly manner. Centralizing management responsibilities in one or a few people requires a reduction in their contributions elsewhere. This is especially true for managing partners. Compensation issues arise not only in valuing the management contributions of a sitting managing partner, but also in compensation during the transition from management back into practice or retirement.

Many managing partners have devoted years tending to the firm's welfare. Illustration 1.3 depicts how the typical managing partner's time is allocated. When it comes time to turn over the reins of authority, they often find that they have watched (and assisted in) the transfer of their practices to other members of the firm. They may be only sixty (or fewer) years old. They may have a substantially reduced practice. Rebuilding at that age is not a prospect thought of fondly. Firms need to consider this typical scenario and provide for "rough justice" in dealing with the post-management period. Failure to do so makes it harder to get old management out and sends the best of the next generation running for cover.

ILL. 1.2 Average Cash Compensation—1994 Managing Partner Survey (1993 Data)

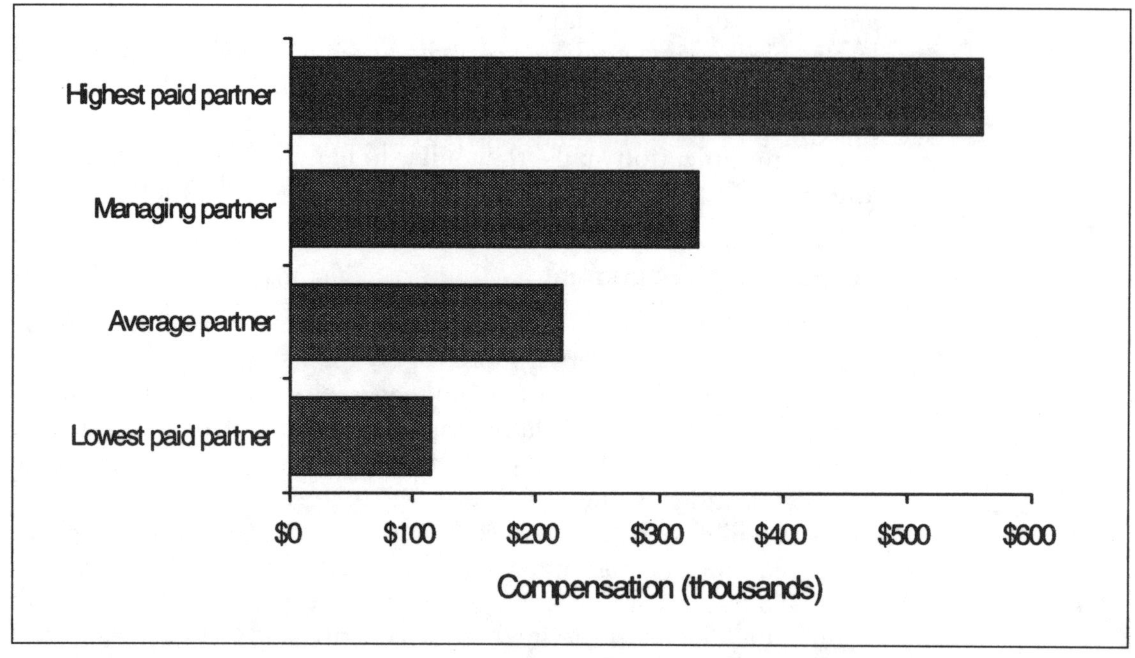

Source: *1994 Survey of Law Firm Managing Partners and Chief Executive Officers.* Altman Weil Pensa Publications, Inc., Newtown Square, PA 19073.

ILL. 1.3 How Managing Partners Spend Their Time

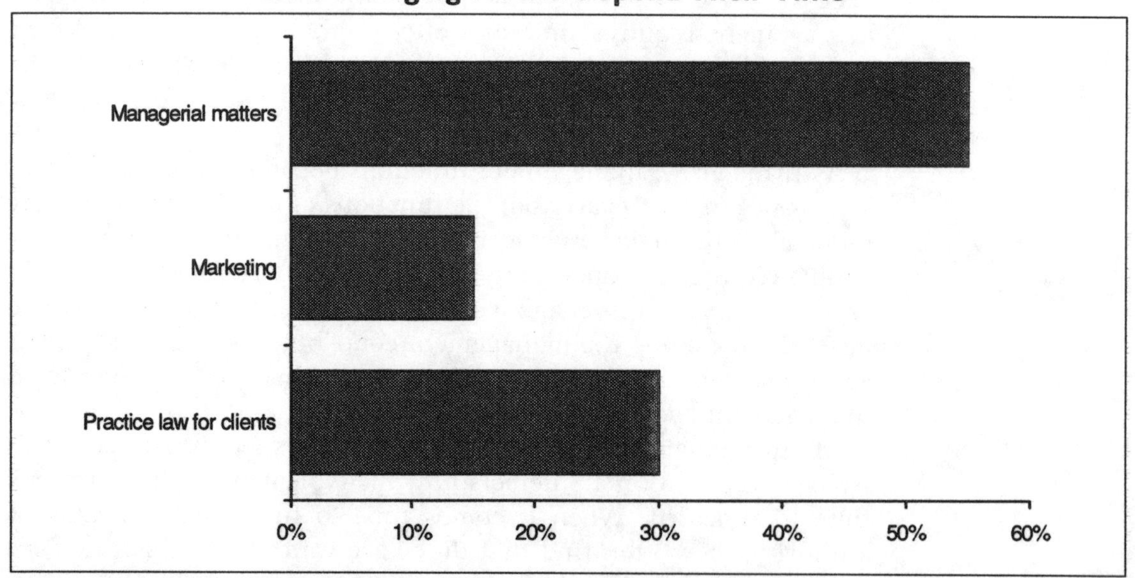

Source: *1994 Survey of Law Firm Managing Partners and Chief Executive Officers.* Altman Weil Pensa Publications, Inc., Newtown Square, PA 19073.

Fees Collected

Personal fees collected was the most important compensable factor formally considered by respondents in our study. Law firms must have a complement of fully utilized fee producers. This includes the partners, who also serve as managers, originators (sales), and owners (risk takers). Although a partner's compensation is not necessarily limited to the amount of his or her professional work that is billed for and collected, a partner's work can have a considerable effect upon the economic results of the firm. This is, of course, more true in smaller organizations than in larger firms. Often overlooked, but an important consideration, is the impact of work performed that is not billed or paid for unless it represented *pro bono* work and was performed in accordance with firm policy.

Law firms have moved to measure fee collections using objective criteria such as working attorney productivity, billing attorney productivity, origination, and portfolio responsibility. Hours or billings fall short for partners, because a partner's responsibility does not end until the bill is paid.

Client Retention

Client retention is often defined as including both client responsibility (the maintenance of good client relations and service even if little work is actually performed by the individual), and case responsibility (the delegation and direction of the effort of others to obtain the best possible results for the client). Responsibility for maintaining the existing client and growing that client's business is acknowledged as a critical element for survival in a competitive market. Many law firms reward the "billing" or "responsible" partner for this client retention function based on fee collections from work done by others. Such reward is often separate from the traditional origination or "sales" function.

Origination (Sales)

The one single factor that establishes the life or death of a law firm is its client base. The "rainmaker"—one who acquires and cultivates client relationships—is the lifeblood of the organization. In any organization, the true "rainmakers" are likely to be the highest paid individuals. The ability to develop and maintain client relationships that serve as a conduit for work coming into the firm is the skill that establishes authority, power, and independence within a law firm. Those lawyers are the net exporters of work to others in the firm.

Participation in Community and Bar Activities

Lawyers are visible members of their communities. Notoriety is achieved through the press reporting on their courtroom skills and their engagements in the political arena. Visibility is also achieved through contributions to civic, volunteer, charitable and religious organizations, community development, and like activities. Such contributions certainly enhance the community; they also elevate the image of the law firm, while simultaneously polishing the subtle, yet important, leadership skills of the lawyers.

In law firms where there is a strong feeling of obligation to the law as a profession, credit may be given for participation in local, state, or national bar association work.

Many law firms recognize the importance of these activities, both in support of the individual's participation and subjectively in compensation. Law is a business of people. The clients primarily engage the individual lawyer. The means to that engagement is often through the relationships established outside the traditional office setting. Also, some firms with specialty practices, which rely heavily on referral work from lawyers, attribute much of the referral work to the friendships that develop as a result of bar association work.

Some law firms, in their pay plans, look favorably on above-average contribution in these areas, some regard it as an obligation meriting no special credit, and a few actually penalize excessive contributions, although they would not be likely to say so.

Profitability

Increasingly, law firms are examining the profitability of their client portfolios. Such examinations obviously look at the revenues generated against the overhead and resources required to service the work. In addition, the firm's strategic and marketing plans come into play as some work is critical in the context of overall firm strategy. Selected matters, practice areas, and clients may support or enable other more lucrative services and must be evaluated accordingly.

A second aspect of profitability involves the acceptance of clients/matters and the fee structures agreed to service the work. In a competitive environment, there is significant pressure to keep the timekeepers fully utilized. It may appear advantageous to accept all work; however, work that cannot be billed and collected has limited value. It is one thing to "get your foot in the door" in pricing initial work, but at some point this investment must begin to show a return.

A third aspect of profitability encompasses the stewardship of partners with billing responsibilities over work-in-progress and accounts receivable. Two measurements are important in this regard. Age of the asset and realization (the percent of the asset ultimately converted into cash) must be examined in tandem. These assets are not like fine red wines that improve with age. Collections, and therefore realization, are improved with frequent, timely rendered bills and diligent follow-up of bills over thirty days old.

Action, or inaction, in these areas can affect every partner's income. The definition of profitability and its measurement can be difficult issues on which to reach consensus among the partners. Therefore, movement in that direction has been slow.

Quality

Some lawyers view quality as an inherent standard that is embodied in seeking the credentials to practice law. Others say that quality is an ethical requirement that is the responsibility of each lawyer. Finally, others say that quality embodies more than just the standards of the profession—quality is also defined by the client.

Quality in the delivery of legal services is undergoing a metamorphosis. A complete discussion of the movement of quality programs through law firms and their clients is outside the scope of this text. However, it should be noted that such programs are making inroads into the legal profession. Law firms and their clients are exploring alternatives in pricing of legal services, delivery of legal services, and training methods, to name a few.

For those firms who are engaged in formal programs, or are considering programs within their firms, the issue of quality in compensation decisions must be addressed. By definition, such programs are never fully implemented or completed. The overriding goal is of "continuous improvement," requiring that the search for quality improvement focuses on increasingly smaller increments.

Compensating excellence in providing quality work product, counsel, and service to clients is in keeping with the *result* clients desire, as opposed to measuring productivity (fees, hours, and the like) which is generally inconsistent with clients' objectives. As law firms embark on partnering relationships with clients, such compensation philosophies will increase in importance.

Productivity

This concept describes the totality of a partner's contributions to the firm and its clients. Partner productivity goes beyond the numbers generated from the firm's time and billing system. It includes the efficiency with which assignments are carried out, the quantity and complexity of work handled, the number of lawyers supervised, the time invested in training, and other firm activities. *Productivity* is a term that goes beyond mere hours or fees. It views a multitude of attributes. Another term gaining in use, with a similar meaning, is *total contribution*.

CLASSES OF PARTNERS

Multi-level ownership structures are not new. However, only about one-third of participants in our compensation systems survey had a second class of owner (40 percent plus, in larger firms). Such individuals shared in profits more often than they shared in voting rights. (See Table 1.1.)

Several years ago, an earlier Altman Weil Pensa study indicated that the prevalence of a second class of partners dropped precipitously below a firm size of seventy-five lawyers, reaching a low of 15 percent for firms of under ten lawyers. As the profession has changed,

TABLE 1.1 **Existence of Second Class of Partners/Shareholders**

By Selected Firm Sizes				All Firms	
2–19 Lawyers		100+ Lawyers			
Number	%	Number	%	Number	%
50	32%	18	43%	137	34%

Source: *1993 Compensation Systems in Private Law Firms Survey*, Altman Weil Pensa Publications, Inc., Newtown Square, PA 19073

smaller firms have searched for a means to satisfy younger lawyers' demands for partnership while preserving or limiting the erosion of profits. (See Table 1.2.)

The authors' consulting experience leads to a caution that when lawyers are placed permanently into special, lower prestige categories, morale problems invariably result over the years. Establishing a lower class of partners as an intermediate step for a limited number of years is often preferable. However, given the economic changes in the profession, some lawyers may never achieve the distinction of full ownership rights. As long as the barrier is established on legitimate criteria that are fairly administered, such an outcome should have minimal adverse consequences.

TABLE 1.2 **Characteristics of Second Class of Owners in Those Firms with a Second Class of Partners/Shareholders**

	By Selected Firm Size		All Firms
	2-19 Lawyers	100+ Lawyers	
	(Number with characteristic)	(Number with characteristic)	Number
Make capital contribution	14	4	30
Same as higher class	2	1	8
Lower, but meaningful	12	1	18
Minimal contribution	3	2	11
Share in part of profit over salary or draw	40	8	86
Vote for senior management	16	5	44
Vote on admission of new members in their class	29	6	59
May serve on firm committees	40	15	116
Can advance to higher owner class	39	17	107
after minimum number of years	12	7	32
separate admission procedure	27	16	89

Source: *1993 Compensation Systems in Private Law Firms Survey*, Altman Weil Pensa Publications, Inc., Newtown Square, PA 19073

After deciding what criteria the compensation of firm owners is to be based upon, the firm must then devise a plan for the administration of the compensation process.

ADMINISTRATION OF THE COMPENSATION PROCESS

Owners at many smaller firms still sit down and discuss an equitable distribution of the pie at year-end, either prospectively or retrospectively. Each partner participates in the meeting at which income distribution is voted on. Because lawyers are generally reluctant to discuss each other's strengths and weaknesses in a face-to-face setting, systems administered by the firm as a whole tend to be quite similar to the lock-step described hereafter. Quite often, partners find such meetings uncomfortable and stressful. It is not the inclination of many lawyers to participate actively in open review meetings; therefore, some firms use closed partner peer reviews. These are written evaluations and are one means of providing broad participative input into a process that works well in many small firms.

Large firms often find such meetings and formal partner peer reviews awkward and time consuming (although some pursue this course if it is in keeping with their culture). As firm size increases, however, so does the use of compensation committees. In some partnerships, a compensation committee is designated by management. In others, general elections are held. A few partnership agreements specify the make-up of compensation committees. Each has its place depending on the personalities involved.

The author's survey shows that the typical compensation committee is three to five elected individuals who can succeed themselves. Compensation committees most often make recommendations to the owners that must be ratified. It is most important that the firm elect individuals who place the interests of the firm above their own personal interests. Compensation committees are used by nearly two-thirds of the participants in our study. For over 40 percent of the respondents, those functions are a part of management.

A few firms charge a senior partner with the responsibility of proposing a distribution of income for each year. This proposal is generally reviewed either by a governing committee or by the firm as a whole, but, typically, it is not often changed. Given the right complement of partners, this system works well.

An alternative process, which avoids confrontations, is the mutual rating system. In this method, income allocations, either in points or percentages, are made by secret ballot of the partners. The ballots are compiled by a neutral party, such as the firm's accountants, or by a consultant working with the firm. In some cases, the high and low ratings are disregarded, and the remaining ballots are averaged. Experience indicates that this process often becomes a proxy for a lock-step system, but not always. The major disadvantage of the system is that adversely rated partners often do not know why they are adversely rated, because there is no feedback. Consequently, the compensation system cannot be used to correct perceived flaws or problems in the activities of partners not rated well. This rating process is obviously a political method, and it is possible that partners will be rewarded for their popularity, rather than for their productivity. Partners who consistently fare poorly in such a process often leave their firms.

A few firms have abandoned the annual compensation ritual, electing instead to review compensation on a bi-annual basis (every other year) or even on a three-year cycle. Such a review period is almost always acceptable to senior partners and is equally often not acceptable to younger partners who look for strong annual growth in earnings. The reasons for this method are to allow for a greater interval of time to elapse, forcing compensation decision makers to consider longer term contributions.

Practice Area Considerations

Practice-specific differences exist. Many intellectual property firms gravitate toward the formulaic and objective end of the spectrum. The lawyers' scientific disciplines and facility with numbers are primary reasons. Insurance defense firms have unique institutional client relationships that require different compensable criteria than a transactional practice. Plaintiff's litigation firms, while transactional, tend to be boutiques, and exhibit high entrepreneurial orientation that needs to be recognized.

Determining Compensation Structure

Firms that see a need to change their compensation systems recognize the dangers of the status quo. Key business developers may take their clients and leave, or highly talented, technically skilled lawyers may be bought at auction. The effect is a loss to the organization and a disruption in the lives and livelihoods of the remaining members.

It is equally true that firms recognize the danger in internally-induced change. For in any closed economic system, a change in compensation will result in some people getting less, while others take more. This perceived danger can block compensation reform within a firm. Prospective change and transition become key elements in the evolution of a compensation system. Change needs to be prospective—looking forward, providing time for the players to adjust to a new rule book or play book. Many firms also take specific action to prevent massive reduction in compensation under a new system. Limits on downward revisions are enacted to protect individual economic circumstances. This step is a major consideration and selling point to mollify insecure partners. Often two, three, or more years may be required to move from the existing system to the new system.

The nature of compensation makes selection of compensable criteria difficult. A successful law firm needs all of the qualities that the various criteria attempt to measure. As always, the individual characteristics of the firm dictate how to blend the ingredients into a successful compensation system. It is possible to reduce the emotion and stress inherent in compensation by understanding that precision and absolute correctness are not attainable. At best, one can create a sense of rough justice, wherein the essential partners are satisfied with the system's fairness, appreciative of the simplicity, and are motivated to work.

Reginald Heber Smith, in a series of articles published in the *American Bar Association Journal* in 1940, defined the objectives of a profit division plan: "The whole purpose is to let the work in the office flow where it will be done best, most quickly, and at lowest cost. The lawyer having too much business must not be afraid to part with it. He must be encouraged to do so, the system must protect his natural and proper interest in the case and the fruits thereof." The objectives of Mr. Smith's system, which was installed at the Boston firm of Hale & Dorr, was to ensure specialization and profitability, and also to reward the individual who was perceived to have an interest in the case. Not all firms would agree with all of these objectives. Further, there is evidence that the statistical system, which Mr. Smith devised and which is discussed later, may work against specialization in some circumstances when it is not installed in the same way as it was under Mr. Smith's leadership and guidance.

Confederation or Team

Relatively little thought is given to the fundamental attitudes that determine how a group of lawyers organize themselves. But the attitudes or views of individual lawyers in the practice shape all facets of behavior—particularly compensation.

Many of the young people who enter law school choose the law as a career because they are independent and value personal achievement. Their college and law school training reinforces individual competitiveness and the ability to master situations independently. When lawyers first enter a smaller law firm, they are generally given responsibilities after a short time and they may receive guidance and training only when they seek it. This freedom reinforces an independent attitude. It is no wonder, therefore, that many organizations of lawyers function as loose confederations of individuals, rather than as organized, disciplined teams. Many lawyers have never considered practicing as part of a true team, much less have they considered the ramifications of association with either a team or confederation type of organization, particularly with regard to compensation.

Whether a firm is a team or confederation is largely a matter of degree. The "pure team" (equal division of profits) or "pure confederation" (space sharers only) are rare.

In a confederation law practice, each lawyer develops individual client relationships. Quite often, there is subtle competition for clients within the office, because serving the more important or better paying clients provides direct rewards and advancement.

Many lawyers are happy only in a confederation environment. They enjoy the sense of independence and the lack of accountability that this organization makes possible. In the confederation approach, each lawyer is viewed as a master of his or her craft and is permitted to practice with little supervision or accountability. The office exists merely to facilitate each lawyer's practice. It provides staff support, a library, occasional research assistance and like amenities, coverage during absence or illness, and companionship. The office, while providing many important aids, is not, however, central to the work the lawyer performs for clients. There is no need for substantial collaboration or cooperation among lawyers.

This form of organization has some obvious shortcomings. There is no central strategy for attracting work. Professional resources may not be optimally used. Specialization is generally neglected. There is a lack of quality control. Training is a stepchild. There is usually little standardization of forms and work habits, because each lawyer basically practices alone.

In a confederation, one is most likely to find a compensation plan based on measures of work production and client origination, which are described later.

A "team firm" is a group of lawyers who work collaboratively to serve clients as a single entity, rather than as a collection of individuals.

Many large law firms adopt some variation on the team approach because the many facets of the legal matters handled are too demanding for an individual attorney to handle alone. But the team approach is available for small firms as well. Team firms are generally recognized by well-defined specialization and by a view of clients as belonging to the firm rather than to any individual partner.

In the smallest group practice, that of two attorneys, the team approach may be manifested by one partner doing all of the litigation and the other concentrating on office work, to the extent that workloads permit. Somewhat larger team firms are generally organized so that all tax, probate, and estate planning is handled by specified individuals, all litigation is concentrated elsewhere, and real estate and corporate work are handled by other lawyers.

This approach to practice requires the subordination of lawyers' individual egos to the recognition that clients are better served by lawyers who are, at least to a degree, specialized and that the lawyers in the firm are all, in their own areas, competent to serve any client.

Team firms do not generally divide income on a pure statistical basis (work produced and clients obtained), although they may require that members work a certain quota of productive hours. Typically, team firms set firmwide standards for the acceptance of assignments, tend to share support staff more easily, and manage members of the firm more closely themselves. Today, team firms also develop firmwide marketing and strategic plans to further the interests of the organization. These strategies call upon all of the talent available within the firm and use each talent to its best advantage.

A "full-service" law firm, to borrow a phrase from the commercial banks, has to be organized in the team fashion.

Prospective or Retrospective Orientation

Overall, U.S. law firms are almost evenly split on a prospective, retrospective, or combined approach as to when the compensation decision is made, according to data from our study of compensation systems. In a prospective system, shares are determined at or before the beginning of the year and apply to that upcoming year. In such systems, a partner will know his or her "share of the pie," but not the size (value) of the share. Everyone has a common incentive to work hard to increase profits because it increases the value of each share.

In a retrospective system, partners' interests are determined at year-end or shortly thereafter. Unfortunately, it has been our experience that these partners have sometimes been unable to file income tax returns on a timely basis because their compensation for the prior year had not been resolved. Shareholders in professional corporations do not have this problem as they will pay a significant tax cost as penalty for not arriving at an amicable decision prior to the end of their fiscal year.

The key advantage to a retrospective system is that it allows the firm to instantly reward superior performance when the money is available. It also provides a tool to lower a partner's compensation if performance lags. Law firms with irregular cash flow, in particular, are more likely to use a retrospective determination of partners' interests.

Many firms prefer to mix these perspectives. The partner's salary or draw may be set at the beginning of the year (prospective basis), considering long-term performance. At year-end, profits after the base compensation are divided by looking back at performance during the year (retrospective basis) and weigh heavily on a single year's performance.

Profit Centers

Profit centers are rarely incorporated into compensation systems, with less than 10 percent of the respondents in our compensation systems study indicating that they use such concepts in compensation. They may be employed to evaluate offices during the integration of a merger or the establishment of a new branch office. Rarely are they used comprehensively on a long-term basis. The most common pitfall in the use of profit centers is that the wrong criteria are measured, resulting in the wrong actions by individuals.

A profit center approach uses cost accounting principles to allocate revenue and expense to individual offices, practice areas, and sometimes timekeepers. Because of the low incidence of this approach, we will not develop its theories and applications. However, because of the complexities inherent in the selection of accounting principles for such systems, the authors recommend that interested individuals obtain *Results-Oriented Financial Management* by John G. Iezzi, published by the ABA. Outside guidance from a CPA experienced in professional service firm cost accounting issues should also be sought.

BASIC APPROACHES TO COMPENSATION

The compensation systems in use in law firms fall into three basic categories:

1. *Subjective*, performance-related systems are those in which the firm, acting through an individual, a committee, or as a whole, reviews the performance of each member, including whatever management information is available, and subjectively determines a relative value for each partner.
2. *Lock-step*, or equal-sharing system, is one in which partners from the same class are advanced together until they reach a full share interest in the firm. In its extreme form, this system eliminates the intermediate steps and all partners immediately share on an equal basis.
3. *Objective*, performance-related systems attempt, through the use of various criteria, to arrive at a numeric value to be used to determine compensation.

A combination of these basic systems is preferred by nearly half of the respondents to our *Compensation Systems in Private Law Firms* survey. Lock-step/equal sharing as a pure system was least preferred, while pure, subjective-oriented systems were ranked second. There are considerable differences based on practice specialty and size of firm. A discussion of the various types of systems follows.

Subjective Compensation Systems

How important are subjective factors in compensation systems in the legal profession of the 1990s? According to a 1993 study by Altman Weil Pensa, Inc., *Compensation Systems in Private Law Firms*, only 18 percent of the law firms surveyed adhere to purely objective (formulaic) compensation philosophies. The remaining 82 percent use subjective criteria in making compensation decisions. In fact, over one-quarter of the firms rely *entirely* on subjective criteria.

One might think that small law firms would tend to be more subjectively oriented. They have the advantage of daily contact among the partners, which tends to make ongoing evaluation and intimate knowledge of everyone's contributions easier to achieve. Extending that logic, one would expect larger law firms to lean toward more formulaic approaches due to the lack of daily interaction among partners. The study, however, found that nearly one-third of law firms with 100 or more lawyers relied solely on subjective criteria for compensation decisions. Second position (29 percent) went to law firms with fewer than twenty lawyers. Nearly half of the firms in the study relied on a combination of criteria, balancing quantitative (objective) measurements of productivity with subjective factors.

Subjective compensation systems embody the concept of "rough justice" or acceptability—that level of relative compensation where you intuitively know that the system is in balance. Individual compensation decisions and overall compensation alignment are "right." It comes from a sense of fair dealing.

Percentages and Points

Traditionally, when lawyers have established new law partnerships, interests have been distributed as percentages. The total of all interests must always add up to 100 percent. Percentages suffer from a psychological impairment where one can advance only at the expense of someone else (a "zero-sum" game). For example, let's say that three individuals start a law partnership with each agreeing to share equally in the profits and losses and each contributing equally to the capital. After a few years, they add a fourth partner to the firm. The fourth partner is to share in 15 percent of the profits or losses and contributes 15 percent of the capital. This leaves each of the three founders with a 28.33 percent interest in the firm. Each capital account must be adjusted to bring the entire system into balance. As the three founders reach the peak of their careers, they are proud of the firm's growth, which they attribute primarily to their skills. However, they are concerned that their ownership and profit-sharing interests continue to dilute with the advancement of each new partner. In addition, many of their younger partners annually grouse at their percentage level. The eventual result is that no one is willing to give up percentages. (see Ill. 1.4.)

ILL. 1.4 Percentage Compensation System

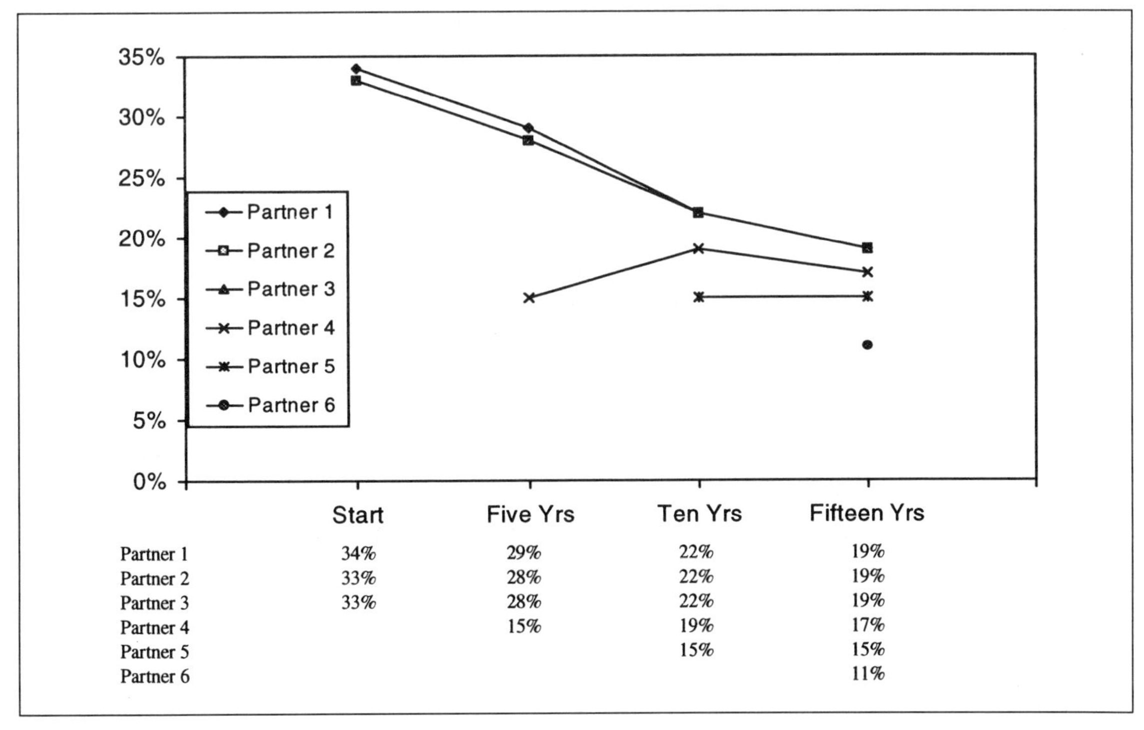

	Start	Five Yrs	Ten Yrs	Fifteen Yrs
Partner 1	34%	29%	22%	19%
Partner 2	33%	28%	22%	19%
Partner 3	33%	28%	22%	19%
Partner 4		15%	19%	17%
Partner 5			15%	15%
Partner 6				11%

Source: Altman Weil Pensa, Inc., Newtown Square, PA 19073.

This is a common scenario. It makes little difference to the participants that each year they have made more and more money. This is because they have increased the value of their interests faster than the dilution impact of growth. Now come the 1990s. The firm's real estate practice collapses. Incomes fall as costs continue to rise and business in other areas remains stagnant. The founders push to maintain their positions and younger partners push to regain lost income. Their only tool is to reallocate the partnership interests, which must still total 100 percent. This is extremely difficult without a pool of retiring or withdrawing partners to recapture percentages from.

Many firms in this situation change to a point system. Rather than artificially remaining at 100 points irrespective of the size of the firm, and reallocating points as new partners are admitted or as younger partners advance, the firm now assigns points on the basis of criteria they develop in order to facilitate a rational compensation relationship among all of the partners. Points are not limited to 100. Frequently, this alleviates the anxiety surrounding individual giving and receiving of points.

A very critical consideration in partner/shareholder compensation is the relation of compensation of one owner to another, in addition to the income of the firm as a whole. The first question is: "What is the desired pay relationship between a newly admitted partner and the most highly paid partner in the firm?" The multiple from lowest to highest can be as little as 1.0 to 1.5 and is frequently 5.0 or higher, depending on the size of the firm, the age distribution within the firm, the amount of profits, the relative control of the firm's book of business, the type of practice, and the aggressiveness of the partners. Larger firms tend toward higher ratios than smaller firms, and insurance defense firms tend to have lower ratios than those firms with a corporate practice, according to data from the annual Altman Weil Pensa *Survey of Law Firm Economics*.

If a low to high ratio of, for example, 1.0 to 4.0 is desired, one could initiate a point system in which the most highly paid partner receives a maximum of 100 points, and the most junior partner a minimum of 25 points. To ascertain the value of each point, it is only necessary to divide the total number of points issued into the sum available for distribution.

The points used should have a significant meaning that differentiates between one number and the next. For individuals who earn large sums of money, a distinction of a few hundred or even a few thousand dollars in compensation per year may be important psychologically to the higher paid partner, but it is meaningless in economic terms. To the lower paid partner there is the continuing question, "How can the compensation system be so precise that it can differentiate by so small a sum?" Law firms have lost productive individuals over such matters, leading to significant morale problems.

In determining the number of points to be used, a firm should consider what significant differentiations it wants to utilize. One can achieve a four-to-one ratio by using a maximum of 20 points and a minimum of 5 points, just as well as by using a maximum of 100 or 1,000. For the individuals between the maximum and the minimum, an additional point should provide a significant amount of earnings.

Point systems are easier to administer than percentages, but are a version of the same method of compensation. Lock-step or equal-sharing systems can also use percentages or points in quantifying the allocation of profits.

The capital accounts of partners under a point system are determined in the same way as those whose firms use percentages. The firm's accountant generally calculates from earned profits to determine a percentage of that total and credits capital accounts with retained earnings in proportion. Additional capital contributions required can also be computed by applying points/percentages to the required total. If a firm wants a different capital account system, it must specify this in its partnership agreement.

How Subjective Compensation Systems Work

How do subjective compensation, or "rough justice," systems work? Some firms approach them in a democratic manner. For example, each partner is asked to participate in the process. The participation may be in the form of a questionnaire or simply narrative comments made during the income distribution meeting. Partners may be interviewed by one or more members of a compensation committee. Ballots or "score cards" may be used where partners provide judgments on other partners' performance in specific areas. The smaller law firms can effectively handle these deliberations in a single meeting. Larger firms may need several months to gather the information and to allow the participation process to work.

Some firms use a committee to perform the evaluation (absent formal participation of each partner). In practice, these committees typically test the waters to ensure that their general thinking is in keeping with that of the firm. Compensation committee reports that contain surprises require significantly more selling to get approved.

When ballots or score cards are used, the firm is actually quantifying the subjective factors in order to provide some methodical way in which to develop compensation decisions. Following are scoring techniques that firms may wish to consider if their own system is not working as well as desired. After scoring, most systems provide for additional adjustment so that inappropriate results are avoided.

Ballot. A ballot system develops rankings by scoring each partner's performance in enumerated areas. Ballots are usually secret. Scoring is often on a scale of one to ten (but any scale will work).

Olympic scoring system. This is a ballot approach where the high and low scores are rejected and the remaining scores averaged. Such a scoring system is useful in offsetting the problem of "outliers."

Determining the median value instead of an average also works, but is more difficult to calculate.

Point accumulation. This is a score card system. Each attribute can have different maximum point values. For example, quality of work may have 25 points, training and development of associates may have 10 points, business development may have 20 points, etc. There is great flexibility in such systems in that a firm is able to change the relative importance of factors as the needs of the firm change from year to year.

Direct assignment. The partners or the committee members are asked to determine each partner's compensation. This method is usually implemented in one of three ways. First, score cards ask for a dollar figure for each partner; the total must equal distributable income. Or, the score card asks for a percent; the total must equal 100 percent. Lastly, each partner may be assigned a point value that may not exceed, say, 50 points; total points awarded for a given partner will usually vary from one score card to another.

Applying Compensation Criteria

Apportioning profit is a complex and difficult task. There are no right or wrong answers. As we often tell law firms, partner compensation is more art than science. Rough justice requires evaluation of the individual, comparing the evaluation against those of all other partners and relating the determinations to available funds. In this part of the process of compensation-setting, the concepts of risk sharing, permitted disparity, and peer group are very important. Each firm will have a different sense of what should be done in these areas.

Risk sharing. How much risk should a younger partner be asked to assume? How does that compare to mid-level and senior partners? In addition, if one's risk is limited, should one's reward be limited as well? If yes, would that still be true in high profit years? These are questions in need of address in a subjective compensation system.

Permitted disparity. We were once asked the question, "Is the individual making $100,000 truly a partner with the individual making $1 million?" It's an interesting question to consider. At what point does the disparity between highest and lowest paid partner become so vast that the concept of partnership breaks down? Are there exceptions? Does it really matter? The answers vary. Generally, in firms of fewer than forty lawyers, once the ratio of the highest to lowest paid partner exceeds 6:1, there is a loss of partnership identity. Larger firms seem more comfortable with spreads in excess of 6:1; their size and operating economics allow for such differences. Often, if you go beyond the one or two highest paid partners, the ratio for the balance of the partners becomes much closer. This is a typical pattern in a law firm with one or two superstar rainmakers.

Peer group. The concept of peer group compensation is simply that because the compensation process is imperfect, it is not appropriate to have small differences in compensation for partners who have small differences in performance. More havoc has been wrought with compensation differences of only a few thousand dollars than one would ever believe possible! The peer group concept is a means to resolve that situation. Individuals with similar overall evaluations are grouped together and all are assigned the same compensation. Compensation gaps between different peer groups are usually significant ($20,000 or more). This strategy is designed to head off second guessing about small differences in compensation.

We stated earlier that rough justice factors should change over time as the firm's needs change. They can also change for a single individual over time. As an example, the younger partner, who feels terribly underpaid at $125,000 while generating $250,000 in fee receipts and having no book of business, may take on a far different view several years later when he or she is controlling $600,000 in business and generating $300,000 in fee receipts. Now it is no longer "fair" to subsidize the younger partners who have no books of business; the more-senior partner must be paid for his or her book of business and the work he or she is performing.

In addition, the younger partner with a family, mortgage, schooling, orthodontics, and no savings feels far less generous about compensation apportionment—he or she is trying to meet everyday obligations and live the appropriate lifestyle for his or her position—than does the senior partner who is more secure and has fewer financial obligations. Each of these individuals will approach the compensation decision differently. Naturally, each is approaching it from his or her own economic situation.

These different positions are often very difficult to reconcile. To start, one must first develop an understanding of each partner's expectations with respect to compensation. One then must then find or create some common ground from which a workable system can be fashioned. Often, the assistance of an impartial individual is required—one who can hear all sides, summarize the issues, and direct the partners toward common ground.

Rough justice is a subjective approach to compensation that, admittedly, requires more effort to implement than does an objective (formulaic) system. For many law firms, however, it is the best way to achieve a perception of fairness and to motivate partners to behave in ways that will lead to the success of the firm as a whole.

Lock-Step or Equal-Sharing Systems

Historically one of the most common compensation methods, lock-step is now one of the least preferred methods to allocate compensation. It is perceived to be out of step with the economic consequences of a maturing legal marketplace. As the post–World War II lawyers approach retirement, more and more lawyers expect to be paid for their contributions on a current basis and are much less willing to carry partners (sometimes even for only a short period of time) whose productivity slips.

However, as with any compensation system, there are advantages and disadvantages to the lock-step system. Partners should have candid discussion of all systems to determine what compensation tenets fit their personalities and relationships. Following is a discussion of lock-step variations to assist with that discussion.

Some law firms develop a system for profit distribution under which partners are given specific income units on admission, and advanced a number of units each year until they reach a determined maximum. For example, a few partners may receive four units on admission, and one additional unit per year, until a maximum of ten units is achieved. In a firm like this, it takes six years from partnership admission to become a full partner.

Such a system is entirely noncompetitive. The system requires only that each partner make an appropriate contribution according to his or her ability, and each is rewarded equally.

On the other hand, such a system is totally lacking in accountability. Once a partner is admitted, progress becomes automatic and no reduction in income share is ever experienced. Such a lack of accountability favors the least energetic, least aggressive, and least capable. It does little to reward hard work, sales ability, or expertise. In such systems, some partners "retire" at their desks long before retirement age, yet they continue to receive a full share.

This type of system can be discouraging to the most energetic partners and to those seeking higher incomes. These partners are frustrated by the small impact their individual efforts have on the overall profit of the firm. This inability to affect their own earnings in any substantial way eventually can lead to a considerable level of frustration, and the loss of some exceptional partners.

A number of refinements can be made to a lock-step system that would improve its acceptability, and preserve its major strengths: simplicity, lack of confrontation, and lack of internal competition (score keeping).

Lawyers' compensation, as previously indicated, typically rises between the 25th and 29th year of practice, then tends to plateau until lawyers begin to retire. The relatively short period in which lawyers, in the hypothetical firm, reach parity means that the firm's practices are out of step with the statistical profile of the profession. One refinement would be to lengthen the time for equal sharing to twenty years of practice. In the process, the number of points used is increased. An advancement schedule could be established in which there is more rapid advancement in the first two years, then a slowing until a full share is reached.

It also would be reasonable for the firm to require partners to work a normal year to continue to share equally in the firm's profits. The firm, therefore, could establish a requirement for a minimum number of billable hours or working attorney collections to be recorded and reported if a partner is to be paid for all of his or her units of participation. The firm could establish a schedule of minimum billable hours, such as: Partners between the ages of 50 and 65—1,400 hours; partners between 40 and 49—1,700 hours; partners under age 40—1,800 hours. A specific budget could be established for "firm" time for those partners with managerial or committee assignments. Authorized management time may be credited, wholly or in part, toward time budgets.

Individual partners who consistently fail to achieve the budgeted hours might have their units of participation reduced, until their effort and shares of profit come into balance. Only disability or the expressed advance action of the firm might excuse a partner from meeting budgeted hours. When an individual accepts a leadership position in a community enterprise, such as a bar presidency or the head of a fund drive, and when the firm approved the activity in advance, a time budget could be set up and made part of the quota.

In addition to establishing accountability for the performance of a certain amount of professional work, an incentive or bonus program can work in conjunction with a lock-step distribution system. Recognition of good work is an important stimulant to productivity and can be used successfully by a law firm.

To provide incentive, the firm might budget an annual fund to be allocated by its policy committee during the last month of the year. The amounts awarded could be specified, say, as no less than $20,000 for partners and the firm administrator, and $10,000 for associates and other exempt support staff. The initial size of the fund might be 5 percent of gross fees collected during the year. The committee may not be required to distribute any or all of the moneys set aside for this purpose.

Minimum award sizes require that the policy committee not simply spread the available funds among all of the partners. The addition of an incentive plan to a lock-step compensation system enables the firm to provide meaningful recognition to those partners whose brilliance or hard work achieves a special result for the firm.

Another means to provide incentive is to permit disparity of plus or minus some percent (say 10 percent) around the lock-step target. The "lock-step range" is then administered by the firm, its management, or a special committee. It is possible to mix additional formulaic criteria or rely on subjective determination to position individuals within the appropriate range.

Objective Distribution Systems

Hale & Dorr

Formula distribution systems were first made popular by the writings of the late Reginald Heber Smith, who was then the managing partner of Hale & Dorr in Boston. These distribution systems are still popular today. To set the stage for discussion, we quote from the pamphlet, *Law Office Organization*, by Mr. Smith, published by the

ABA in 1943. The material first appeared in the *American Bar Association Journal* in 1940.

Every partner has a percentage or share of profits; those shares must total 100 percent. If a partner is entitled to be increased by 1 percent, some other partners must be decreased by 1 percent and that is where the rub comes. This is best overcome through records which are impersonal, but which indicate plainly what adjustments among partners are in order.

It has been our experience over a number of years that all such adjustments can be made in good spirit and without rancor, in a very brief space of time, and by unanimous vote of all partners *provided* thorough and painstaking work has been done in advance by the manager (the managing partner).

All the records that show what every partner has done exist. They need only to be assembled. At the end of the fiscal year four facts about each partner are known:

1. What he has received from the firm (his drawing allowance plus his share of profits for the fiscal year).
2. What he has contributed to the firm through work (this is the total of his "prorated" earnings plus any time charged to the firm).
3. What he has contributed to the firm through business brought in (this is the total of bills sent out during the fiscal year in cases in which he was responsible attorney, less any bills that went to "bad" during the fiscal year).
4. What he has contributed to the firm through the profit on such business (this is the excess of bill over cost, less the loss when cost exceeds bill or the bill has gone to "bad" during the fiscal year).

Just as partners' shares in profits are expressed in percentages, so these figures must be converted into percentages.

This can be illustrated by assuming a firm with four partners, using round figures, and we will do the sum for Item 2—Work Done.

Partner	*Value of Work Done*	*Percent*
A	$20,000	50.00%
B	10,000	25.00
C	7,500	18.75
D	2,500	6.25
	$40,000	100.00%

Exactly the same thing is done for business credit and profit credit. Again, this will be illustrated by using the same four partners.

	Business Credit		Profit Credit	
Partner	Amount	Percent	Amount	Percent
A	$20,000	40%	$ 4,000	40%
B	15,000	30	2,000	20
C	10,000	20	3,000	30
D	5,000	10	1,000	10
	$50,000	100%	$10,000	100%

We think these three different kinds of contribution by a partner to the firm are not of equal importance. We think work done is most important, business credit next, and profit credit last. To reflect the different degrees of importance we "weight" the percentages. (Any firm is entitled to come to its own decision about this and to use any weighting it likes.) Work done is weighted at 6 (multiplied by 6), business credit is weighted at 3 and profit credit at 1. The total is divided by 10. The result is still a percentage figure and that figure we call "Value Produced." The following table shows the mathematics.

	Work Done		Business Credit		Profit Credit			Divided by 10 Gives Value Produced
1	2	3	4	5	6	7		
Partner	%	x6	%	x3	%	x1	3 + 5 + 7	
A	50.00	300.0	40	120	40	40	460.0	46.00
B	25.00	150.0	30	90	20	20	260.0	26.00
C	18.75	112.5	20	60	30	30	202.5	20.25
D	6.25	37.5	10	30	10	10	77.5	7.75
	100.00%	600.0	100%	300	100%	100	1,000.0	100.00

What each partner has received from the firm is reduced to a percentage and that figure is called "Value Received." Let us also make that computation:

	Received from the Firm	
Partner	Amount	Percent
A	$10,000	40%
B	6,000	24
C	5,000	20
D	4,000	16
	$25,000	100%

The manager's report will end up with two final figures for each partner—i.e., "Value Produced" and "Value Received." Statistically, each partner has produced more than he has received or has received more than he has produced. In the former case he has a credit and in the latter case a deficit. We can now state these final figures:

Partner	Value Produced	Received from Firm	Credit	Deficit
A	46.00%	40.00%	+6.00	
B	26.00	24.00	+2.00	
C	20.25	20.00	+0.25	
D	7.75	16.00		-8.25
	100.00%	100.00%	+8.25	-8.25

There are ups and downs in law practice so that a one-year record is too short a time on which to base a judgment. Hence, exactly the same figures are made up in cumulative form and embracing all years for which we have these records.

These two tables (one giving the annual and the other the cumulative figures) are typed and a copy goes to every partner. He thus has the whole story and he has exactly the same evidential material as has the manager. The manager writes and sends to each partner a short report suggesting that one or more partners have their shares in profits increased and others accept decreases. The partners meet and customarily the report is accepted without debate. That fixes the share in profits of each partner for the *next* fiscal year. Having gotten over the tough part the partners then relax and enjoy a squabble over whether the youngest junior (i.e., associate) shall have any raise in pay and if so, how much.

As to juniors, the manager prepares somewhat similar tables, but they are simpler. Figures about juniors need not be converted into percentages and there need be no weighting. The record sets out what each junior has earned by work done (measured by prorating), business credit, profit on such business, hours worked, value of hours produced (hours worked multiplied by cost per hour) and present salary.

It can readily be argued that all the qualities and values of a lawyer cannot be caught in a statistical net no matter how finely spun. That allegation is conceded. But the question is: "What better method is there?" It is impersonal, it is open and aboveboard, it does yield a vast amount of information, and it has been assembled in the manner which the partners themselves have decided to be as fair as they can make it and which they have incorporated into their partnership articles. After prescribing the method, the partnership articles do not say that the statistical tabulations are conclusive, but that they shall be considered "as substantial evidence."

> The figures are not given literal application. If a partner has a credit (excess of value produced over value received) of 2 points, that does not mean that he shall at once have his share of profits increased 2 points. But if, year by year, the partner has been maintaining a credit, it is evident that he should have some increase.
>
> Furthermore, anyone who deals with such figures is bound to be impressed by the fact that while the figures for one year are an adequate base, the cumulative figures as they are kept year after year grow progressively more accurate until they do approximate the truth and afford an adequate basis for judgment by a group of partners whose intention and desire is to deal justly with one another.
>
> With their internal affairs settled, the partners can depart on vacation . . .

Although Mr. Smith collected data, he and his firm did not directly apply that information to compensation. That, however, is the course some law firms have adopted. If compensation is to be determined on the basis of value of work done, business credit, and profit credit, consideration must be given also to the other factors that are compensable—those factors that are listed earlier in this chapter. In particular, credit must be allocated for management of the firm and for training associates and staff, or these functions will be neglected.

For the firm that wants to have specialists, implementation of a formula-based income distribution system may make it difficult to maintain specialties. Areas of law that are perceived to be lucrative, in that they pay more than the base hourly rate, will be sought after by all attorneys, regardless of their training. Service areas, such as estate planning and some aspects of tax work, might be avoided if they pay at less than standard value.

The allocation of credit for business obtained is difficult. In the first year in which a new client is served by the firm, it is usually possible to allocate a credit clearly to an originating partner or associate. But when client A sends in client B to an individual who is not the originator of client A, a problem arises. When a client has been in a firm for a good number of years and has been served by many of the firm's lawyers, there is also a question as to allocation of credit. Obviously, unless all of the lawyers have served the client well, the client might long be gone from the firm. This raises a question of how long sales credit should be allocated to the originating attorney. Some firms have resolved this by giving a less highly weighted credit for client maintenance once the client is established within the firm—for example, after a period of three to five years.

There are other problems in assigning sales credits. Some clients come to a firm because of its general reputation, not because of a specific lawyer. How will such clients be credited? Will credit go to the lawyers who happened to be called by the receptionist, or will there be a "firm" credit?

To a considerable degree, credits for bringing in clients and, to some degree, production credits, can be manipulated. In some firms, it is not unusual to find credit in the partner production column for work actually performed by a secretary or legal assistant (and occasionally by an associate). The associate's time might later be written off to training, while the supervising partner gets full work credit.

Credit systems of every sort skew lawyer behavior, just as the tax laws skew economic activity. And just like the tax laws, not all of the resultant behavior can be anticipated when a plan is adopted, nor is all of the activity beneficial.

Profitability can be measured by comparing the fee with the value of time at standard rates, but this can be distorted when inexperienced personnel are assigned to a case and their time is then written off. On the other hand, care must be taken that the responsible lawyer is not penalized because he or she has agreed to use a case for training a fledgling lawyer or paralegal.

Law firms that wish to allocate credit for business obtained generally develop an extensive set of rules for crediting the function. Such rules may provide for division of origination credit between two or more partners claiming the credit, and may set limits on the time frame over which the credit is awarded.

A set of rules is also required with respect to the crediting value of work done when more than one lawyer is involved in producing the fee. The basic fee structure of most law firms recognizes that lawyers are not of equal value. Table 1.3 shows the relationship between hourly rates and years of experience, based on the first admission to practice law.

TABLE 1.3 **Standard Hourly Billing Rate by Years of Legal Experience as of January 1, 1993**

Years of Experience	*Average*	*Median*
Under 2 Years	$ 96	$ 90
2–3 Years	108	104
4–5 Years	120	115
6–7 Years	131	127
8–10 Years	143	140
11–15 Years	158	150
16–20 Years	168	165
21 or More Years	181	175

Source: *1993 Survey of Law Firm Economics*, Altman Weil Pensa Publications, Inc., Newtown Square, PA, 19073.

Based on this data, a lawyer with under two years of experience would need nearly two hours of work to obtain the same value that a lawyer with 21 or more years of experience receives for one hour of work. When fees are not charged at standard value the difference must be allocated. In many firms this allocation is done *pro rata*, as shown in Table 1.4.

In some firms, the assisting lawyers and paralegals are credited at standard hourly rates, and the responsible or billing attorney gets whatever is left. In others, billing partners are given full discretion in allocating credits on their matters.

In the system described by Mr. Smith, weighting factors are given as six, three, and one, but it is noted that other firms may weight the three factors differently. Giving only twice as much weight to producing work as to obtaining it places a high value on the sales function. Firms with an established clientele may want to place greater emphasis on getting the work done. Firms in a start-up situation, or firms with a desire to expand or with a predominantly transactional practice may, on the other hand, give a greater weight to producing clients. Once a system of weights is established, however, it is difficult to change. Some parties will fall into the role of producing work, while others excel in bringing in clients. When a change in weighting is proposed, somebody's ox is gored, and consequently, change is resisted. This may mean that the firm's incentive system may not be current with the firm's real needs.

Another decision that must be made is whether credits are allocated when a bill is sent or when a bill is actually paid. Those firms that use a computer may find that they have little flexibility with respect to this. Most computer systems erase the underlying billing information once time has been translated into an invoice. When profits are at stake, of course, it is far better to allocate actual receipts. After all, it is fee receipts that are being distributed under the system.

TABLE 1.4 **A Method for Dividing Credit for Doing Work, Based on Time Records and Standard Hourly Rates *(Partner's standard hourly rate is $150.00; Associate's standard hourly rate is $65.00)***

Attorney	Hours Recorded	x	Hourly Rate	=	Time/Dollar Value	=	% of Total
Partner	3	x	$150	=	$450	=	68.7%
Associate	3	x	$ 65	=	$195	=	30.3%
Total					$645		100.0%

If the actual fee collected is $500.00, credit Partner with 69.7% (i.e., $348.50); credit Associate with 30.3% (i.e., $151.50). If the fee collected is $900.00, credit Partner with $627.30; credit Associate with $272.70.

One year doesn't make a career, and the numbers produced in one year should not alone determine compensation for the following year, as Mr. Smith points out. Few firms, however, want to be burdened by the accumulation of data for the whole history of the organization. Consequently, many firms use a moving average generally of three, four, or five years when formula measures are employed.

As can be gathered from the foregoing, formula compensation systems can become quite complicated and expensive to administer. Appendix I is an example of the complexity of one law firm's formula plan.

Work Purchase

Some law firms use an alternative credit system to that described above. It is sometimes referred to as "The Purchase of Work System." In this system, the lawyer who obtains a client is regarded as the manager of that client's work. In this role, the lawyer may call on the services of any part of the firm. The originating lawyer is expected to use those people in the firm most capable of handling the client's problem at the lowest price.

If an obtaining lawyer does not want to handle legal work for which he or she is approached, he or she may find another lawyer within the firm who wants to manage the matter. In this case, the lawyer turns total responsibility and all credit over to the other attorney.

Each lawyer and paralegal is assigned a standard billing rate for each year. The manager of a file "buys" time from other attorneys and paralegals at his or her own discretion at a percentage (such as 85 percent) of the producing lawyer's and paralegal's standard rate. The manager is then free to set a billing rate for the client at any rate above or below the standard rate, depending on all of the billing factors. Contingent fee work is also charged to its "manager" at a percentage of standard rate. Time records are kept by all lawyers and paralegals on a client-by-client and case-by-case basis.

Each of the firm's partners who has a managerial responsibility for the firm is assigned a budget of hours for management activities, including the training of associates and paralegals. Lawyers are credited in the system for such activities at a percentage of standard hourly rates.

Retainers paid in advance are credited to the account of a responsible partner when received, and debited when funds are reallocated to other attorneys who have performed services. Figures are accumulated for all producing personnel, including associate lawyers and paralegal assistants. Partner-managers do not get the free use of income-producing personnel of the firm. When a matter is completed, or at the end of each year, the account of the responsible attorney is adjusted so as to deduct all credits allocated to other attorneys and legal assistants.

If the manager of the case expends more professional effort than the fee justifies, he or she may end up with a "loss," resulting in a reduction from his or her accumulated credits. If, on the other hand, the matter is billed at more than standard fees, there may be a large excess (premium) of credit over and above the percentage called for by the discounted standard rate. In most firms, associate lawyers are not permitted to be the billing attorneys, and, consequently, are limited to providing services at a percentage of standard rate.

This system encourages the use of the most efficient people and the use of specialized talent. It offers ample reward for the individual with the ability to bring in clients, without giving that person any incentive to personally perform the most highly paid work and to farm out the less well-paid activities.

The work purchase system does not encourage training or other administrative/managerial activities because such activities reflect only a discounted rate value. In addition, partners lose the ability to generate leveraged profits and the potential for premiums from billable work if time is invested in discounted firm activities. It also concentrates much of the work in the firm on a few good people, and could adversely affect the morale and economic health of the firm as a whole. It may restrict access to the firm's resources by junior partners or others without sufficient clout.

Profit Center Approach

As indicated earlier, profit center approaches to income distribution are found in only about 10 percent of firms. However, they represent another variant of the objective or formulaic philosophy.

This concept typically arises in confederation-type law firms, where there is some sentiment among the partners that the costs of production of different types of legal services, by different attorneys, vary dramatically; where there is an absence of strong, centralized management; and where there is an atmosphere of competition among partners. The profit center approach is characterized by an allocation of fees and overhead among various partners or groups of partners within the firm, and a resulting allocation of profits among partners assigned to each of those groups.

A pure profit center approach results in the creation of a number of "firms" within the organization, each sharing overhead items in various proportions. A pure profit center approach is almost always divisive, and does not encourage specialization or transfer of work between members of the firm. It rarely works in the best interests of clients of the firm and almost always results in disputes over fee and overhead allocation.

"Modified" profit center approaches are used in some firms whereby the performance of various profit centers is used to determine distribution of a portion of firm income, with the remainder being distributed either equally, or in accordance with another parameter, such as seniority. Modification of the profit center approach in this way provides some degree of interest in the overall performance of the firm, and reduces the divisive effect of the system. Other modifications include interdepartmental allocation of revenues to reflect the cross-selling of other departments (i.e., one profit center originates the client or matter and another profit center handles the work). However, even modifications such as these rarely overcome the problems inherent in this approach to paying partners and shareholders.

Tiered Systems

Some firms allot a base dollar amount for each owner. It may be called a draw or a salary. If there are funds available for distribution after all base amounts are paid, such funds are usually not distributed in accord with the relationship of basic amounts to each other. At one extreme, for example, funds available for distribution may be allocated equally among the partners. That type of system will provide a very considerable incentive for all partners to ensure the firm's profit. Generically, these systems are referred to as "tiered" compensation systems.

Sometimes there are various "pots" of funds available for distribution. For example, if the base compensation amounts to the first $500,000 of distributable funds, the next $100,000 might be shared equally, and amounts above that, or above $600,000, might be distributed in some other way. The final pot may be distributed on the basis of production, peer evaluation, a determined point or percentage interest, or in many other ways. Tiering of this type enables a law firm to provide various incentives.

Sometimes there are specified requirements for participation in amounts above the base draw or salary. Such requirements may be based on billable hours of work, bringing in business, or meeting other predetermined objectives. In other situations, tiers are used to provide younger partners with a greater interest in the profits of the firm beyond its current base.

CAN A PARTNER'S VALUE BE MEASURED?

Valuing partner contributions, for purposes of compensation, staffing, retirement, and the like, is a challenging and emotional issue. Altman Weil Pensa, Inc., has frequently advised clients that it is not possible to measure empirically the value of a partner's contribution, either over the short term or over the long run. However, if we are speaking about pure economic value, the authors have begun to conclude that such value is fundamentally determinable by a complex mathematical formula, and that the factors that are not explicitly included in the formula, but arguably give rise to value are, in fact, implicitly included or largely irrelevant. Consider the following.

The Basic Formula

Years of consideration of this issue have led the authors to the conclusion that the fundamental formula is:

$$P = M_a(C_r - C_w) + R_p(C_w + V_f) - O$$

where:

P = Individual partner's economic value

M_a = Margin on associates

C_r = "Responsible" attorney credits of the individual partner

C_w = "Working" attorney credits of the individual partner

R_p = Firmwide realization on partner revenues

V_f = Value of individual partner time expended in firm-authorized efforts, at standard rates

O = Per lawyer overhead

In effect, the formula states that a partner's economic value is measured by the economic value of revenues generated by his or her individual efforts on behalf of clients, plus profits generated by associates on matters managed by the partner, minus the partner's individually allocated overhead. All credits in the formula ("C" factors) are measured on the basis of fees received. Time worked is irrelevant if not revenue-generating, unless the firm itself is willing to pay for it, out of revenues that otherwise would be shared by those partners who generated them. "O" factors are also calculated on a cash basis.

That said, let us explore some of the individual factors.

Margin on Associates

"Margin on associates" (M_a) refers to profit on work done by associates, calculated on a cash receipts basis. Paralegals can be included in the margin calculation if desired, which means their compensation is removed from overhead for purposes of computing margin. If paralegals are not included, they are treated as part of overhead. Not including them simply increases both responsible attorney credits and working attorney credits, as well as per-lawyer overhead.

M_a is the sum of associate working attorney credits on fees received, minus their combined compensation and allocated overhead, as a percentage of their combined revenues. Overhead for these purposes may be computed firmwide on a per-lawyer basis, or if paralegals are included, separately for lawyers and paralegals, or if substantially different for partners and associates, separately for each, or even individually calculated for specific groups of lawyers (in a particular department, for example), or for each individual associate and paralegal, if necessary.

In effect, $M_a = [\Sigma C_{wa} - S_a - (O_a \times A)]\ \Sigma C_{wa}$

where:

ΣC_{wa} = aggregate associate working credits

S_a = associate salaries and benefits

O_a = per associate overhead

A = number of associates

Responsible Attorney Credits

"Responsible Attorney Credits" (C_r) are the combined effect of both originating and managing/billing partner. If a firm tracks origination, C_r is the full value of all matters both originated and managed (billed) by the partner, one-half the value of matters originated by that partner, but managed and billed by another, and one-half the value of matters originated by others, but managed and billed by him or her. If the firm does not track origination, C_r is simply the value of billing partner credits, measured on a receipts basis.

The formula assumes that origination and management of legal matters are equally important. In today's environment, that is probably a fair evaluation. However, if necessary, a different relationship can be incorporated into the formula.

Working Attorney Credits

"Working Attorney Credits" (C_W) of individual partners also are measured on a cash receipts basis. This concept is employed in most law firms, but can be controversial, depending upon how allocation of fees is made on multiple-lawyer matters. This can be done:

- At the discretion of the billing attorney (in which case, most discounts will result in writing off of all associate time, while maintaining full value of partner time);
- On a pro-rated basis, whereby the computer automatically calculates the discount to be applied to the value of each lawyer's work, whether partner or associate, based on relative time values;
- Or, as we believe is often the best approach, whereby associate time first is credited at standard rates, and partners assume credit for whatever balance remains, be it a discount from standard rates, or a premium.

Regardless of which method is used, it needs to be applied consistently within the firm. Otherwise, C_W is going to mean very different things for different partners.

Realization on Partner Revenues

The concept of R_p, "realization on partner revenues," is the key to operation of the formula. It takes into account the value of firm time, authorized and for which partners are accountable, on both management and marketing, including recruiting, training of associates, business management, practice management, firm marketing (other than individual rainmaking), *pro bono* work, and the like, all at each individual partner's billing rate. It implies the firm's ability to delegate, provide authority, specialize, and require accountability for these functions. It is not applicable to things all partners are expected to do, or where certain functions are equally spread among all partners. The concept considers the fact that if specific, identified partners did not, for example, manage the firm or its departments, others would have to do it, and, therefore, the "economic opportunity cost" of self-management must be spread among all. This factor reduces the economic value of revenues attributable to the work done (working attorney credits) of each partner by the economic opportunity cost of otherwise billable hours spread through the firm. The R_p factor is essentially the summation of working attorney credits divided by those credits plus the economic value of authorized firm credits, at standard rates.

In effect $R_p = \Sigma C_w \div (\Sigma C_w + \Sigma V_f)$,

where:

ΣC_w = aggregate partner working credits

ΣV_f = aggregate authorized firm credits

Overhead

The last factor, overhead (O), can be computed on a per-lawyer basis for the firm as a whole. If there is a substantial difference between overhead allocation to partners and associates, it can be computed separately for each, and used on that basis in the different components of the formula. Remember, paralegals should not be included in overhead if they are treated separately in the M_a calculation.

Assumptions

Key assumptions of the basic formula to determine a partner's value include the following:

1. Associate margins are substantially the same throughout the firm. *If not, they can be computed separately for each department, or even for each associate.*
2. Paralegals can be considered associates for M_a computation, although in that case overhead for purposes of that computation may become "overhead per nonpartner fee earner."
3. Firm time is credited in C_f only for official, individually assigned functions, for example: managing partner, executive committee, business development committee, recruiting, training, departmental management, and the like. Time commitments of each will be different, and may be limited to a budget, in some cases.
4. Overhead per partner is not substantially different than overhead per attorney. *If so, it can be computed separately for each.*
5. All matters are managed/billed by a partner.
6. Origination and management of legal matters are equally important.

The formula can be adjusted to reflect an individual firm's economic realities with respect to assumptions 1, 2, 4, and 6, but not for 3 and 5.

Countervailing Arguments

The primary argument against determining a partner's economic value by formula is that the formula does not measure the value of seniority, bar and community activities, management or training contributions, teamwork, cooperation, and the like. These arguments are only partially apposite.

One could argue that seniority is irrelevant, as senior lawyers generally are charged at higher rates, and arguably should be generating more business for others to do. After all, which is more valuable: a seventy-five-year-old lawyer who generates no business, but is fully productive as a working attorney, or a thirty-five-year-old lawyer who generates well over a million dollars a year worth of business for himself and others to do?

Bar and community activities are likewise questionably relevant outside of public relations opportunities, except in instances where they generate new business, or the firm has authorized their expenditure and is willing to credit all or part of the time at standard hourly rates to the lawyer involved. After all, how important is it for a firm to have a partner who is president of the state bar association if it generates no business? The authors would argue it is only as important as one's partners believe it to be, in which case they can pay him or her for it, at standard rates. Or at least credit the individual with the hours expended in achieving that, at standard rates, recognizing that not only might it result in economic value (and probably income) to that partner, but also in a reduction of the economic valuation of each hour's worth of dollars collected for client work done by the other partners in the firm, under the rationale that were it not done by one partner, the firm would ask another to do it.

As a result, the formula induces a new level of scrutiny to economic (and nonrevenue-producing) activities pursued in a law firm environment.

Uses of the Concept

The concept of a measurement of economic value of a partner might be used for a number of purposes. They include the following:

1. Evaluation of an existing partner compensation system, to determine its economic validity;
2. Providing a basis for *commencement* (only) of compensation review, by a compensation committee;
3. Determining the value of a "book of business" being brought by a lateral partner;
4. Adjusting economic performance of individual partners to improve overall firm economic performance; and
5. Identifying the need for improvement of associate margin or partner realization, and measuring the effects of such improvement on individual partner incomes.

The economics of law practice are changing, as Altman Weil Pensa, Inc., consultants have been prognosticating for years. Greater partner accountability is going to be necessary, both from an economic perspective, as well as from that of quality, management, client relations, and marketing. The formula outlined above arguably provides a starting point for consideration of the age-old question, "What is each partner really worth to this firm?"

PURE GRINDERS AND FINDERS: THE THEORETICAL VALUE OF RAINMAKERS AND SERVICE PARTNERS

Who is more valuable: the rainmaker who cultivates clients or the partner who does the work? This question has perplexed and befuddled law firms for decades. Both rainmaking and lawyering are clearly important to the long-term future of the firm. But how does one measure the relative value of such contributions when deciding how to divide the partnership pie?

Pure lock-step systems have ignored the question. Some formula systems, most notably the pure Hale & Dorr System, have attempted to take both activities into account, but leave the relative weighting of "finding" versus "grinding" to guesswork. The truth is that both activities are important, but neither alone can be considered to be the full measure of a partner's contribution to the firm. By focusing on the two extremes—pure "grinder" and pure "finder"—the authors explore how each archetype contributes to the earning power of the law firm and offer suggestions for how those in charge of setting compensation should value such contributions.

The Pure "Grinder"

The archetypical service partner—one who originates no business of his or her own—contributes to the profits of the firm through personal labors on behalf of the clients of others. In reality, this partner might also contribute by delegating to and supervising the work of associates (which would add value), but for purposes of this analysis we shall assume the contribution is solely that of a performer of legal work.

In any given year, a grinder's economic contribution is measured by the excess of the cash collected for services over and above cash compensation (including benefits and perks) and the administrative cost of supporting his or her efforts (i.e., secretarial help, rent, and occupancy, etc.). For example, consider a new partner (male for ease of pronoun reference) with the following profile:

Age	33 years old
Billable hours	1,800 per year
Hourly rate	$150 per hour
Administrative cost	$100,000 per year
Cash compensation	$100,000 per year

If one assumes that the firm can bill and collect 100 percent of the value of his billable hours, the partner's economic contribution to the firm in his first year is as follows:

Hours	1,800
x Rate	x $150
= Revenue	$ 270,000
– Administrative Cost	– 100,000
– Compensation	– 100,000
= Contribution	$70,000

In essence, this hypothetical partner has generated sufficient revenue to cover his support costs, pay his compensation, and still leave $70,000 on the table for others to share. On the surface, one might easily conclude that this partner has superstar qualities and is probably undercompensated by as much as the amount of his excess contribution. Yet, to evaluate the partner's contribution properly, one must look beyond the results in the first year.

In any single year, it is conceivable that a pure service partner might generate remarkable numbers. But partnership is a long-term commitment and compensation systems need to take into account economic contribution over the long term, not simply in any single year. (The only exception to this rule is the firm that operates on an "eat-what-you-kill" profit center compensation system, one that is probably better regarded as an office-sharing arrangement, rather than a law firm in the true sense.) There will be some years in which the partner contributes excess values and others in which the firm will "carry" him. One hopes that, over the course of a partner's career, the excess dollars created will balance out with the costs of "carrying" the partner in years when his contribution is on the decline.

Analysis of the long-term compensation prospects for this hypothetical service partner requires constructing a simple economic model and using it to determine how much the firm can afford to compensate the partner over his entire career, if the years of excess contribution are to completely offset those years in which his compensation and overhead exceed the revenue he produces. In theory, the model is a "zero-sum game" in which all gains (i.e., years of excess contribution) are exactly offset by losses (i.e., years in which the partner is "carried"). In constructing the model, consideration is given to the fact that billable hours tend to decline slowly with advancing age. In addition, it also reflects the effects of inflation on the firm's hourly rate structure and its administrative costs.

Simply stated, the model measures the cumulative contribution of the partner over his career and seeks to determine a percentage increase in compensation that will fully distribute all excess values (i.e., drive cumulative contribution to zero) by retirement age. It assumes that the partner builds excess values early in his career and gradually takes them out of the firm later in his career. It is also based upon the somewhat generous assumption that the firm is able to recoup all of the inflationary increase in administrative costs by increasing the partner's hourly rate.

The initial assumptions of the model are as follows:

- Partners are admitted at age thirty-three and retire at age sixty-five.
- The partner's work pace will gradually decline over his thirty-two-year career from 1,800 billable hours to 1,200 billable hours by age sixty-five.
- In the firm's hourly rate structure, a new partner's rate is $150 per hour. It rises by a constant percentage each year to top out at $300 per hour for the most senior partners.
- Overall administrative costs increase at the rate of 4 percent per year.

If the partner receives no increase in compensation above his $100,000 base, his career excess contribution could be as high as $3.7 million. This, of course, is unrealistic, because one expects compensation to continue to increase, at least in line with inflation. The interesting question is, "How large a percentage increase can the firm afford to pay the partner each year so that he is able to take out all of his excess contribution to the firm?"

The somewhat startling conclusion of this analysis is that, under the assumptions set forth above, the very best the pure-service partner can hope for is an increase of a little more than 4.5 percent per year—only a half percent better than the assumed rate of inflation! There are probably many thirty-three-year-old partners currently making $100,000 to whom the prospect of retiring at age sixty-five earning $400,000 per year might seem quite attractive. With inflation at 4 percent per year, however, it amounts to treading water for thirty-two years.

Certainly some of this model can be adjusted to create a more favorable projection, but there is probably no combination of reasonable assumptions, except for a dramatically increased level of billable hours, which would allow for compensation much in excess of the rate of inflation.

The inevitable conclusions from this analysis are as follows:

- If the only contribution a partner makes to his or her firm is to work hard for much of his or her career, the best the partner can hope for in compensation is to stay slightly ahead of inflation.
- To dramatically improve his or her lot, the partner must either work much harder and longer or find other ways to create incremental value.
- Over the long term, every dollar of excess contribution generated by a partner from his or her own billable hours will have to be used to fund his or her compensation.

To the extent that higher operating costs and increased partner compensation can be passed along to clients in the form of higher rates, the firm can afford to pay the partner more, but client resistance to higher rates limits the firm's ability to do so. Cost control or reduction programs may also provide some room for increasing compensation, but one runs the risk of cutting costs so low as to impair the partner's ability to function effectively. The inescapable conclusion is that partners must find ways to create value over and above the value of their own hours if they are to earn pay increases appreciably better than the rate of inflation.

Creating additional value can be done in a number of ways. Development of standard work product, exemplars, substantive practice systems, and other techniques that increase productivity and create the opportunity for billing more than standard time value are some examples. If there is more work available to the partner than he or she can comfortably handle, delegating to and supervising associates are other effective ways to create additional value. Of course, developing profitable work for high quality clients is probably the best way to create value.

The Pure "Finder"

Most firms look to business origination either individually or as part of a team effort as the primary way for a partner to create excess value. But is there such a thing as a pure "finder"—one who performs no legal work per se but functions only as a business originator? How much can a law firm afford to pay for pure origination?

If the answer to this question is to make sense, one must first accept the earlier premise that the best a pure service partner (i.e., one who has no origination of his or her own and works only on "firm" clients or clients of other partners) can hope for in terms of percentage increases in compensation, is a rate roughly equal to (or only slightly better than) inflation. That premise implies that the profit on all partner hours billed and collected must go to pay the partner and build future values to provide for the time when his marginal contribution is negative.

For purposes of illustration, assume the following:

- All lawyers, except the rainmaker, bill and collect an average of 1,600 hours per year.
- Service partners bill at an average rate of $200 per hour.
- The rainmaker's hourly rate is $300.
- Administrative support expenses for partners and associates are $100,000 and $75,000 per lawyer, respectively.
- Benefits and payroll taxes are 15 percent of salaries.
- Operating leverage is maintained at 1.5 associates per partner.
- There are three classes of associates whose billing rates and salaries are as follows:

Associate Class	*Billing Rate*	*Salary*	*Profit @ 1600 Hrs*
Senior	$150	$80,000	$73,000
Middle	$125	$67,000	$48,000
Junior	$100	$50,000	$28,000

The first and simplest case is one in which a partner has no billable hours, but is able to generate enough work to keep one and one-half associates busy. Assume that the associates are at the senior level.

Scenario 1, as depicted in Table 1.5, shows that unless he generates billable work for himself, the rainmaker can expect a maximum compensation of only $9,500 from his or her $360,000 book of business. The scenario gets much worse if one assumes that the associates are in the lower profit categories. (An interesting aside relates to the situation in which a firm is asked to give up a percentage of fees to an of counsel for access to $360,000 worth of business. In this example, the firm cannot afford to give up more than about 2.6 percent of the total "book" without incurring a loss, if the of counsel costs $100,000 to maintain. Most law firms give away the store in this area.)

It is unrealistic, of course, to expect that a rainmaker will have no billable time at all.

TABLE 1.5 **Pure "Finder"—Scenario 1**

	Head Count	Hours	Rates	Income and Expense	Percent of Revenue
Firm Income					
Rainmaker	1	0	300	$0	
Service partners	0	1,600	200	0	
Associates—senior	1.5	1,600	150	360,000	
Associates—middle	0	1,600	125	0	
Associates—junior	0	1,600	100	0	
Revenue	2.5	960[1]	150	360,000	100.00%
Firm Compensation Output					
Assoc. salary—senior	1.5		80,000	120,000	33.33%
Assoc. salary—middle	0		67,000	0	
Assoc. salary—junior	0		50,000	0	
Benefits (% of salary)			15%	18,000	5.00%
Overhead—associates	1.5		75,000	112,500	31.25%
Service partner compensation	0		0	0	
Overhead—partners	1		100,000	100,000	27.78%
Total costs				350,500	97.36%
Available for rainmaker compensation				$9,500	2.64%
Operating leverage				1.5 to 1	

[1]Average hours per lawyer.

If the rainmaker also generated enough work to provide himself 1,000 hours, for example, the firm could afford to pay him up to $309,500 for his $660,000 book of business. If the rainmaker's hours were 1,500, his compensation could go as high as $459,500 for a book of $810,000. Eventually the rainmaker's compensation has to top out, however, unless he is able to continue leveraging himself with more and more associates.

In the above example, each additional senior associate the rainmaker keeps busy creates an additional $73,000 in value available for compensation.

The most counter-productive scenario occurs when the rainmaker's top senior associate is admitted to partnership. If operating leverage is to be maintained at 1.5 to 1, admitting the senior associate to "service partner" status creates a requirement to find work for 2.5 additional associates!

Table 1.6 illustrates how Scenario 2 might work out if a rainmaker generated no hours for herself.

In this case, assume that the three associates are split evenly among the three classes.

TABLE 1.6 **Pure "Finder"—Scenario 2**

	Head Count	Hours	Rates	Income and Expense	Percent of Revenue
Firm Income					
Rainmaker	1	0	300	$0	
Service partners	1	1,600	200	320,000	
Associates—senior	1	1,600	150	240,000	
Associates—middle	1	1,600	125	200,000	
Associates—junior	1	1,600	100	160,000	
Revenue	5	1,280	143[1]	920,000	100.00%
Firm Compensation Output					
Assoc. salary—senior	1		80,000	80,000	
Assoc. salary—middle	1		67,000	67,000	
Assoc. salary—junior	1		50,000	50,000	5.43%
Benefits (% of salary)			15%	29,550	3.21%
Overhead—associates	3		75,000	225,000	24.46%
Service partner compensation	1		220,000	220,000	23.91%
Overhead—partners	2		100,000	200,000	21.74%
Total costs				871,550	94.73%
Available for rainmaker compensation				$48,450	5.27%
Operating leverage				1.5 to 1	

[1]Average blended or effective rate per lawyer.

Scenario 2 permits the rainmaker to generate excess value of $48,450 as compared to $9,500 for Scenario 1 but she must generate an additional $520,000 of new business to make it happen.

To some extent, these two scenarios are not comparable because the associate staff mix differs. Comparing "required origination" and "available values" under the two scenarios assuming varying levels of rainmaker hours and that all associates are at the middle level yields other interesting results, as shown in Table 1.7.

If the practice will only support 1.5 to 1 leverage, the rainmaker must contribute two or three times the business book to support herself and a service partner. And she creates very little excess value in doing so. Is it any wonder why niche practices are difficult to force beyond the "threshold" stage of one partner and a "comfortable" number of associates?

Properly stated, the conclusion for this analysis is as follows: The most a law firm can afford to pay a rainmaker over and above the profits derived from his or her own billable hours is the marginal profit derived from the associates that he or she is able to keep busy, irrespective of how many partners he or she occupies.

These examples and scenarios are meant to be provocative. In reality, especially in the short run, rainmakers can produce excess values, especially if the firm is in an asset-driven posture (i.e., has more lawyers than are needed to service the work available). One can argue that the rainmaker is getting no credit for sopping up excess capacity among partner and associate ranks. That argument may play in the short run, but as a long-run strategy it will not work because it never allows the firm to ask the tough question: "Who are these people and why are they here?"

The analysis is also based on assumptions about associate staffing that, if changed, could produce better results. For example, if the rainmaker used only senior associates he or she would fare much better because the profit margin on senior associates is higher. The tradeoff for that, of course, is a higher average hourly rate and higher cost to the client.

TABLE 1.7 **Comparison of Scenario 1 and Scenario 2**

	Scenario 1A		*Scenario 2A*	
Rainmaker Hours	***Required Origination***	***Available Values***	***Required Origination***	***Available Values***
0	$300,000	($28,075)	$ 920,000	$ 43,850
1000	600,000	271,925	1,220,000	343,850
1500	750,000	421,925	1,370,000	493,850
1800	840,000	551,925	1,460,000	583,850

Final Observations

These illustrations are meant to be extreme. Yet, one often has to go to extremes to make a point. The inescapable conclusions are:

- Law firms cannot afford too many pure "service partners." All partners must contribute excess value in some way, either by supervising associates (permitting greater leverage), creating opportunities to bill more than the time value of the work, or making a contribution to business development.
- Rainmakers must produce their own billable values to justify higher compensation.
- Admitting pure "service partners" puts an extraordinary burden on firm rainmakers—a fact that they have not willingly accepted nor generally understood in the past.
- The most valuable partners are those who offer a balance of skills: worker, delegator, supervisor, and rainmaker.

OTHER OWNER COMPENSATION ISSUES

Distributions

In a partnership, partners may be assigned drawing accounts that represent a prospective share of profits (as defined in a partnership tax return). This means that, if there is a shortfall, some of the drawings will have to be repaid to the firm. Shareholders and professional employees of professional corporations may be assigned salaries. The term implies that the full amount is earned and none of it is returnable. A salary, however, may be withheld by the firm if cash flow is insufficient to cover all overhead and shareholder compensation. Many law firms, partnerships, and professional corporations alike got into trouble in the late 1980s by borrowing to sustain owner compensation when cash flows began to falter. See the related short piece in Appendix 2 that discusses the impact of law firm borrowing on compensation.

The amounts to be paid to owners should be agreed to and time of issue regulated. In some law firms, partners are permitted to obtain payments at their own volition. This can make a law firm's finances disorderly. Some partners may draw out (and do draw out) more than they are entitled to, leaving nothing for the others. Furthermore, such an arrangement tends to create havoc in the bookkeeping office. It is not possible to plan cash flow needs if partners can demand funds at any time.

Further, salaries and draws should be conservatively set. It is desirable to provide for cash reserves to cover cash flow imbalances throughout the year or for an unexpected dip in profits. It is easier on the firm and the workers if paychecks are not missed and capital calls can be avoided. Concurrent with this theme, conservative salaries and draws force some measure of discipline on the owners' lifestyles. It can help prevent overextension if the firm's numbers falter. Finally, if the firm is desirous of a successful incentive-based income distribution plan, it must make the incentive payments significant in relation to overall compensation. Conservative base compensation is a means to achieve that end.

Special distributions or bonuses may be paid at any time that management determines that it has an adequate reserve of cash to meet its needs and some for contingencies. Generally, law firms pay out profits to owners quarterly or annually. The deciding factor appears to be the form of organization. Partners need to make quarterly estimated income tax payments and they tend to distribute profits in accordance with those cycles. Shareholders usually do not need to make quarterly payments as they have income tax withheld from each paycheck. Professional corporations, therefore, tend to bonus on an annual basis.

Tax Treatment of Partners and Shareholders

Partners are self-employed individuals. The partnership is not a separate taxable entity, but rather a pass-through entity from which items of income and loss, deduction and credit pass to the partners.

Shareholders are employees. The professional corporation is a separate taxable entity. It can pay tax and will if income is left in the corporation at year-end. An exception is a professional corporation that has elected to be taxed as a partnership ("S" election). In that instance more-than-2-percent shareholders are treated as partners with respect to the application of fringe benefits.

There are differences in the way such compensation is treated for tax purposes and the way it is most likely reported by an owner. Comparisons between shareholder and partner compensation must be made with care to ensure that an "apples-to-apples" analysis is performed.

In partnership accounting, partner profits include payments made for health, disability, and life insurance and pension. For example, a partner with a $200,000 share of profit may experience a cash flow of:

Paid out to insurance benefits	$ 6,000
Contributed to pension plan	$ 30,000
Paid out in cash	$164,000
Reportable earnings	$200,000

The partner could deduct the amount paid into the pension plan, 30 percent of the self-employed health insurance premiums (1995), and one-half of the self-employment tax she owes on her individual income tax return.

If this same individual were a shareholder in a professional corporation, her reported income would be $157,471. At first glance, it would appear that the shareholder was paid less. This is not the case. An earnings summary explains why:

Earnings Summary for ______________
(Year ending December 31, 1994)

Salary and bonuses paid (reportable earnings)	$157,471
Group life, health, and disability insurance premiums (paid by firm not reportable as income)	$ 6,000
Medical reimbursement plan payments (paid by firm not reportable as income)	$ 1,000
Pension plan contribution (paid by firm not reportable as income)	$ 30,000
FICA taxes paid by employer	$ 5,529
	$200,000

It is important for all employees to receive such a statement so that the individuals understand that there is considerable investment beyond the salary and bonus.

SUMMARY

As law firms move through the 1990s, a decade that in nearly everyone's opinion promises to be much tougher economically than the 1980s, many are re-examining their systems for compensating partners. With the expectation that there will probably be less to pass around, there is a growing interest in moving toward objective merit-based systems that are integrated with individual partner goal-setting and peer review programs. Pure lock-step and formula systems are giving ground to more consciously managed systems that are based upon a combination of both subjective and objective observations, and which recognize compensation as an important motivational factor in professional practice.

The migration toward managed systems for partner compensation has occurred gradually over the last decade. Lock-step and formula systems alike, while they retain some of their basic structures, have been modified to allow for more conscious slotting of partners. Movement up the lock-step ladder each year is no longer guaranteed and some partners are being frozen in place or moved down. Formula-driven systems have become less rigid with the introduction of bonus pools and other devices, which allow firm managers to adjust for the aberrations that formulas inevitably create.

The new merit-based systems require that managers develop a clear statement of the subjective and objective measures of partner performance, ensure that the criteria are consistent with the firm's strategic objectives, and forge a broad consensus among the rank-and-file partners in support of the criteria. It also requires that they have a clear understanding of how different partners contribute in different ways to the economic success of the firm. While business development skills are important, especially in a recessionary economy, many firms may be overcompensating rainmakers. Others may be overcompensating partners who originate no business, but instead service the clients of others. Understanding the economics of the two types of activities is essential to developing a balanced system of partner compensation. Compensation systems in the 1990s must reflect these economic realities. Above all, firms will have to strive to build cadres of partners with balanced skills: lawyering, managing, and rainmaking. All three are equally important to the long-term success of the firm.

NOTE

1. Managing partners invested 55 percent of their time attending to the business affairs of their law firms in 1994, up from 47 percent in 1992 according to a study of large law firm managing partners. *Survey of Law Firm Managing Partners and Chief Executive Officers, 1994 Edition,* Newtown Square, PA 19073, Altman Weil Pensa Publications, Inc., 1994.

CHAPTER 2
Of Counsel Compensation

OVERVIEW

Look at a sample of law firm letterhead or listings in Martindale-Hubbell and you will usually find lawyers listed as "of counsel." In the late 1960s the significance of the listing was usually quite clear. It meant, "Here is a former partner who is either retired or is scaling down toward full retirement."

But things were much clearer and simpler in those years before the bull market for legal services. Mega-firms had 100 lawyers. The entirety of Martindale-Hubbell fit into two volumes. Law firms were old-fashioned partnerships based upon common law conventions.

With the rapid growth and maturation of the legal market, there has evolved a need for a title that describes something other than the traditional partner or associate relationship between a lawyer and his or her law firm. Now one sees a variety of titles in use, such as "senior attorney," "special counsel," "senior counsel," or the elegantly simple "counsel." Each different title presumably signifies some kind of relationship other than the traditional ones, but the lack of standardization of terminology leaves one at a loss to divine precisely what the law firm means by making the distinction. In many cases, the lack of clarity has been intentional.

At least, however, the title "of counsel" has emerged as one with definite—albeit broad—significance. In practice, "of counsel" has been used to mean one of two states of practice:

1. One that is in transition, or,
2. One that is segregated from the mainstream practice of the law firm.

The most common uses have been to signify:

- That a partner or former partner has retired or is scaling down to retired status. This is probably the purest use of the title to describe "transition."
- A "living-together arrangement," under which a lateral partner candidate and the law firm are operating, while each scrutinizes

the other and ponders the prospect of eventual full partnership status. This usage incorporates both concepts of "transition" and "segregation" in that there is an expectation that the lawyer's status will eventually evolve into full partnership.

- That a lawyer's practice has been isolated from the firm for ethical or business reasons. For example, certain states require that lobbying activities be isolated from other practice areas so that partners who do the lobbying work do not share fees with others who may have an economic interest in the outcome of legislative developments. In other cases, the lawyer or the firm may want to maintain permanent of counsel status to create separate profit centers for division of profits or other business purposes. Similarly, a lawyer may wish to retain independent contractor status to retain certain advantages under the tax law. This usage is purely one connoting segregation.
- That the lawyer in question is a specialist practitioner who has a referral relationship or is "on call" to the firm, and perhaps may have similar relationships with other law firms. Once again, the usage is purely to connote segregation.

On May 10, 1990, the Standing Committee on Ethics and Professional Responsibility of the American Bar Association adopted and issued Formal Opinion 90-357 which governs when and how law firms use the title "of counsel." In doing so, the committee also included the most common variations on the theme of of counsel listed above.

Successfully creating an of counsel relationship does require both parties to do their homework and to be very thorough and careful in how they agree on the terms of the relationship. For starters, all such relationships should be governed by a written contract between the parties.

At a minimum, the agreement should cover the following:

- The purpose of the relationship and both parties' expectations as to benefits to be gained;
- Specific duties and responsibilities of both parties under the agreement;
- The term of the agreement and conditions under which it is subject to extension or renewal;
- Guidelines for client acceptance, work allocation, client billing protocols, and control of files;
- Agreements as to ownership of intellectual property and files;
- The method of compensation, including timing of payments;
- Conflict-checking policies and procedures;
- Provisions by which either party may terminate the agreement;
- Consequences of termination of the agreement with respect to unfinished work in progress, uncollected fees, retention of files, re-use of intellectual property, continuing contact with joint clients; and

- Indemnification terms and conditions, confidentiality provisions, and any other rights of either party that are retained or limited.

OF COUNSEL COMPENSATION

Compensating of counsel requires a discussion of overhead allocation, fee attribution, funding of joint promotional expenses, and the like. Many firms will provide for a very simple structure, while others will engage in more complex arrangements. The best approach is very much dependent upon the nature of the of counsel arrangement.

Scaling Down

If the arrangement is one where an existing partner is scaling down to retired status, then there is an opportunity to append the of counsel compensation structure to the firm's existing partner compensation program.

A very simple approach is to define expectations for reduced workloads with corresponding reductions in compensation. The following depicts an institutionalized program used to wind down a partner to retired status:

> "The of counsel position is a period of transition for the individual and the firm. Of counsel status usually is a five-year period of steadily declining direct contribution to the benefit of the law firm in terms of hours, with a changing focus away from billable work and new business development toward external and internal relations. Each of counsel may propose a scheduled wind down that meets personal needs and those of the firm. The firm will approve such proposals provided that it is in the interest of the firm and not detrimental to the firm's mission of serving its clients. The general thinking of the firm in this regard is:
>
> | | |
> |---|---|
> | Year one (Age 65) | 90% of 2500 hours = 2250 hours |
> | Year two (Age 66) | 75% of 2500 hours = 1875 hours |
> | Year three (Age 67) | 60% of 2500 hours = 1500 hours |
> | Year four (Age 68) | 40% of 2500 hours = 1000 hours |
> | Year five (Age 69) | 15% of 2500 hours = 375 hours |
> | Year six (Age 70) | Fully retired |
>
> Compensation will be adjusted downward in proportion to the reduced commitment (i.e., Age 67; 60 percent commitment; compensation 60 percent of pre-wind down levels)."

If the firm uses a point/percentage system, the number of points/percentages is reduced. If the firm wants to lock in the payments, it could set forth a salary schedule for each year.

It is important to provide the opportunity for additional compensation for business origination or other contributions that materially exceed the agreed-upon expectations.

Living Together Arrangements

This form of of counsel incorporates both concepts of transition and segregation. It is important that the compensation arrangement yield a result that will allow the individual to be inserted into the firm's partner compensation structure at the end of the "break-in" or "getting-to-know-you" period.

Most typical is an agreement that provides for an assumption of overhead and a percentage of fees produced. Fee allocations vary based on the source of the business and who performs the service:

1. Of counsel originates and services the work.
2. Of counsel originates and the firm services the work.
3. The firm originates and of counsel services the work.

It is preferable to compensate based on fees collected. However, issues of adjustments (premium or discount), allocation of payments to fees and costs, and billing protocols must be determined and set forth in the agreement. A transition cut-off should also be provided that stipulates how matters billed but not yet collected will be handled when the of counsel is brought into the firm as a partner.

Isolated Practice

This type of arrangement represents a pure segregation of practices, either for ethical or business reasons. It is, therefore, imperative that the economic arrangement comply with the segregation intent of the arrangement.

Overhead should be divided into basic direct and indirect costs. Direct costs should be absorbed by the parties on a transaction basis. Indirect costs should be shared by the parties on some reasonable basis (square footage, per lawyer, per fee-earner, per partner, or per capita) or some weighted allocation method. Fees can be allocated using a breakdown as shown above in the living together example.

Referral Relationships

This is another example of a segregation arrangement. However, for this arrangement, specific overhead allocations are not important for the compensation agreement. They are important, however, for compensation negotiations.

In this instance, the firm is engaging a specialized resource. Compensation can be a percentage of fees, an hourly rate, a fixed fee, or a combination of pricing alternatives that is mutually acceptable.

A very important aspect in of counsel arrangements is the general requirement that the individual not be an employee of the firm. For practical purposes, it means that the of counsel is responsible for all tax payments (FICA self-employment, income, and the like), benefits, and other insurance needs. Responsibility for such coverage as professional liability, health, life, and disability insurance should be clearly set out in the agreement. In addition, the firm should notify its carriers about such arrangements to ensure that the firm is adequately protected.

CHAPTER 3
Associate Compensation

OVERVIEW

The term *associate* is applied in this text to include those lawyers employed by a law firm in a full-time capacity without any attributes of ownership. It includes the traditional associate—a lawyer in his or her first five to ten years of practice and on a career track to an ownership interest—as well as the new breed of associate that is not on the career track to partnership.

Law schools, no matter how prestigious, produce not skilled lawyers, but well-schooled graduates. The art and craft of lawyering is learned by observing and doing during several years of training. Law firm training has historically been a profit center for law firms. Then, starting salaries were quite low (as were the billing rates) and clients paid for the training as the young lawyer worked on matters. Today, economic conditions have changed dramatically. As law firms struggle with current economics, they are torn between several issues: the problem of maintaining leverage, the fungibility of associates and some partners, the difficulty of transferring client work over to other personnel, and the changing characteristics of the workplace that have altered the work ethic of the nation. Partners can no longer assume that associates will work evenings and weekends, even if the work is available.

Law firms are moving toward a more efficient system to deliver legal services. Process reengineering supported by technology, coupled with client-defined quality, and focus on the client's objectives, places a strain on both the need for young lawyers and the concept of training as a profit center. In fact, most clients are resistant to paying for the training of younger associates. Many clients require staffing plans (with individual credentials) for engagements. Inexperienced staff are usually excluded by the clients.

In fact, during the highly touted 1980s, law firms required three to six years to break even on the cash-flow deficit of the first full year of an associate. Even on the accrual basis it would often take into the second year to reach profitability. Table 3.1 depicts profitability of an associate moving through the first six full years of practicing law as well as for associates overall.

TABLE 3.1 Associate Profitability—First Six Years

	Years of Experience						Associates as a Group
	Year 1	*Year 2*	*Year 3*	*Year 4*	*Year 5*	*Year 6*	
Fee production							
Avg. annual billable hours	1,788	1,819	1,855	1,853	1,842	1,890	1,822
Avg. standard billing rate	$104	$111	$113	$123	$127	$136	$121
Fee production	$185,952	$201,909	$209,615	$227,919	$233,934	$257,040	$220,462
Avg. time written off on all associates	($18,381)	($18,381)	($18,381)	($18,381)	($18,381)	($18,381)	($18,381)
Billable fees produced	$167,571	$183,528	$191,234	$209,538	$215,553	$238,659	$202,081
Cash receipts							
Holdover		$70,239	$76,928	$80,158	$87,830	$90,352	
Carry forward	($70,239)	($76,928)	($80,158)	($87,830)	($90,352)	($100,037)	
Cash receipts	$97,332	$176,839	$188,004	$201,866	$213,032	$228,974	$202,081
Position costs							
Avg. overhead[1,3]	$87,640	$87,640	$87,640	$87,640	$87,640	$87,640	$87,640
Avg. total compensation[2]	$61,032	$66,265	$68,213	$73,909	$77,461	$84,105	$74,318
Position cost	$148,672	$153,905	$155,853	$161,549	$165,101	$171,745	$161,958
Profitability							
Cash basis profit (loss)	($51,340)	$22,934	$32,151	$40,317	$47,931	$57,229	$40,123
Cash basis cumulative profit (loss)	($51,340)	($28,406)	$3,745	$44,062	$91,992	$149,221	
Cash basis margin	–52.7%	11.4%	15.3%	17.7%	20.5%	22.3%	18.2%
Accrual basis profit (loss)	$18,899	$29,623	$35,381	$47,989	$50,452	$66,914	$40,123
Accrual basis cumulative profit (loss)	$18,899	$48,522	$83,903	$131,892	$182,344	$249,258	
Accrual basis margin	10.2%	14.7%	16.9%	21.1%	21.6%	26.0%	18.2%
Pipeline calculation[4]							
Avg. unbilled time	$46,155	2.6 months					
Avg. accounts receivable	$43,594	2.4 months					
Total pipeline	$89,749	5.0 months					
Avg. gross receipts (AGR)	$214,115						
Total pipelines/AGR	41.9%						

[1]All amounts are on a per-fee earner basis.
[2]Total compensation includes cash, benefits, retirement contributions, and employer taxes.
[3]Average overhead includes all firm expenses, except lawyer and paralegal compensation.
[4]Pipeline reflects the delay in cash receipts attributed to timekeeping, billing, and collection policies. This is reflected in the cash receipts "Holdover" and "Carry forward" rows.
[5]Source: *1994 Altman Weil Pensa Survey of Law Firm Economics*, Altman Weil Pensa Publications, Inc., Newtown Square, PA 19073.

All this leads to the conclusion that being an associate is no longer a simple apprenticeship period prior to becoming a partner. Nontraditional associate lawyer positions—senior associate, staff associate, off-track associate, and the like—are more likely to have careers that end short of the ownership position.

The primary purpose of the associate is to work on the partners' matters and to generate a profit for the firm. Associates are rarely employed to generate a book of business (although this is, or should be, the prerequisite for advancement). The rule of thumb, even today, is that an associate should generate billings that are three times his or her compensation. For most firms, this is not the case. Setting compensation on this basis will have unintended consequences for the firm. For example, Table 3.1 depicts the cash and accrual basis profitability of young associates. Only in the later years does profitability reach 20 percent (just about when some firms make the associate a partner).

In the 1980s, large law firms, flush with transactional work for which large premiums could be had, bid up the starting salaries of recent law school graduates. The upward pressure eventually affected the bulk of the profession. The unchecked upward spiral stopped in 1989 with law firm starting salary offers hitting a peak national median of $50,000. There it has remained through 1993. Corporate law departments, who traditionally hire experienced lawyers, have lowered starting salary offers for the comparatively few recent graduates in each of the past two years.

Associate compensation had been a competitive battle with law firms actively watching the "market" or "going rate" for the associates they required. They were less concerned about the economics as they would pass the cost on to the clients. Now, although the firms are still watching the external market, decisions are based more on the economics the position can support.

Beyond the starting salary, associate signing bonuses, historically common, are now provided by about only one-fourth of law firms. Eligibility for such bonuses varied greatly depending on the years of experience and size of firm. However, the amount of the bonus seemed pegged at a median of close to $3,000 in 1993.

Once the associate is on board, the firm must have a system to evaluate the performance of the individual. While the first few years of practice may be more of a lock-step advancement system, after that, individual performance differences begin to surface and must be recognized. Performance evaluations are very often granted third-class importance, relegated to the "necessary but evil" paperwork of the firm. This is the wrong approach. Evaluation is critical as a component of the training program, the compensation program, and the admission to ownership program. A few firms have found that improper evaluation techniques have come back to haunt them when disgruntled employees take their employer (or former employer) to court. Technology can greatly assist in simplifying, leveling, and enhancing the evaluation process. Although outside of the scope of this book, interested readers should contact Altman Weil Pensa, Inc., to learn more about computer-scored associate evaluation programs.

Law firms tend to evaluate their associates using the same criteria that are used for the partners. There are several reasons for this. First, the partners are familiar with the definitions and have agreed as to their importance and meaning within their firm. Second, the associates are hopefully on a track toward eventual ownership and need to be evaluated against that goal. There is no better preparation than the criteria the partners apply to themselves. Third, it is relatively simple to apply the standards as the requisite data is already available.

In practice, the relative importance of criteria changes as the associate gains experience. In the early years, the partners look for work ethic, ease of training, and willingness to learn, as well as other factors that determine the person's ability to "fit" in the firm. As experience is garnered, the partners look more at how legal knowledge is applied, effectiveness of client counseling, knowledge of clients' industries and businesses, client rapport, efforts to develop business, and community contacts and interests. In the years just prior to formal consideration for partnership, such attributes as client development, business acumen, willingness and ability to assist new personnel, and leadership skills take on added importance.

Throughout their tenure, associates are evaluated on how well criticism, difficult situations, and demanding clients are handled. Of course, the evaluation also must consider the level of fee receipts produced and how efficiently they are generated.

SALARY ADMINISTRATION

Salary levels vary around the nation. Factors such as size of firm, population density, geographic region, and practice specialty all impact salary. For example, smaller firms tend to pay less than larger firms, less populated areas tend to pay less than large cities, and the west (except California) and west central regions of the U.S. tend to pay less. Readers are encouraged to participate in and purchase the surveys that report associate compensation. Such surveys are regularly conducted by the authors and others. Compensation varies significantly by location, size of firm, and other factors that are usually reported separately in surveys. In this way, one can profile compensation data against many factors to gain a sense of the market in which they compete. Table 3.2 is an example of the variability of compensation and the different variables one will consider.

As in most employment, experience is a significant factor in compensation advancement. Lawyer experience is measured from the standard first year admitted to practice law in any jurisdiction. The range in associate median compensation starts at just over $50,000

TABLE 3.2 **Selected Associate Compensation Data[1]**

	Lower Quartile	Ninth Decile
West Central	$51,134	$75,180
Northeast	63,598	119,999
Under 9 Lawyers	44,241	97,467
Over 75 Lawyers	65,287	114,999
Under 100,000 Population	46,205	81,994
Over 1,000,000 Population	64,323	114,999
Plaintiff Trials	39,080	92,167
Patent	75,116	137,143
One year of experience	50,469	86,933
10–14 years of experience	70,830	116,016

[1]W-2 plus employer paid benefits and payroll taxes.
Source: *1994 Altman Weil Pensa Survey of Law Firm Economics*, Altman Weil Pensa Publications, Inc., Newtown Square, PA 19073.

and peaks at almost $83,000 (See Illustration 3.1). However, associate compensation is not an endless series of increases. At some point compensation reaches an upward limit that is difficult to overcome. This is primarily due to the fact that associates should not be profit takers (although some firms allow them to be). As such, they face real economic limits if they sell primarily time (8,760 total hours in one year, some of which even the most aggressive biller must reserve for other activities) with rates already under careful client scrutiny.

Salary is the most important component in an associate's compensation package. After salary comes health, disability, and life insurance. Bonuses are important, but current firm economics have diminished their frequency and value. Pensions are rarely appreciated by younger employees, particularly young professionals.

There are three primary approaches to salary administration. The first focuses on the years of experience, the second on a career track, and the third on individual contribution (performance). The early years for some firms are purely lock-step because of the inability of firms to distinguish among the attorneys while they are learning the basic skills of serving client needs.

Years-of-Experience Salary Administration

This approach essentially creates a class-oriented compensation structure. Each year the individual advances along the compensation schedule. How far the individual progresses from year to year will vary based on performance, the differential for the year, and any movement of the entire schedule.

When establishing the initial pay scale, the firm must first determine its market and where it wants to position itself in the market.

ILL. 3.1 Total Compensation—Associates (By years since admission, all firms 1993)

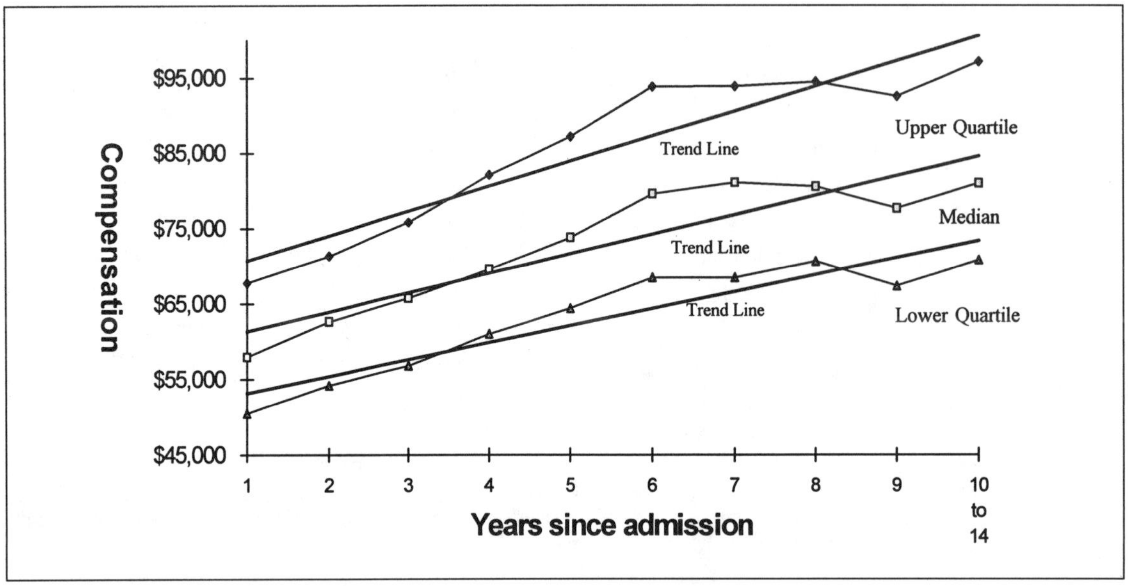

Source: *1994 Survey of Law Firm Economics*, Altman Weil Pensa Publications, Inc., Newtown Square, PA 19073.

In the introduction, we discussed the concept of a labor market. Each law firm must assess the market in which it competes for associate talent. For most firms it is a regional market. Once the market is determined, survey data should be obtained that can provide information regarding prevailing wage levels in that market or as close a proxy to that market as possible. Based on the market data, the firm should position itself to compete. For example, many employers like to be in the inter-quartile range (the middle 50 percent). This leaves the bottom 25 percent of prospects as not meeting the standards of the firm and the top 25 percent for someone else. Other firms apply the 80/20 rule and seek to include 80 percent of the market. Here, they will structure themselves between the 10th and 90th deciles, leaving the 10 percent of the market at either end to others. Still other firms seek to employ fewer yet higher caliber associates. They might want to position themselves in the market between the median and ninth decile.

After the firm positions itself in the market, the firm must examine the client base and other matters to determine the economic realities of its practice. If the firm can reasonably expect to generate $171,000 (1,800 hours at $100 with 95 percent realization) of fees from this position and the fee-earner overhead (say $87,000), pension (none initially), benefits (say $5,000), and taxes (say $4,000) equal $96,000, then the salary offer cannot exceed $75,000 dollars just to break even. Most likely, the firm would need to pay a $50,000 to

$55,000 salary for such a position, leaving a profit of only $25,000 (a 15 percent margin) to $30,000 (an 18 percent margin). So much for the "rule of threes" that would say compensation of $57,000, overhead of $57,000 and profit of $57,000 on fees of $171,000!

Combining the two analyses described above provides the firm with an indication of the market it can compete in and the economically justifiable offer it can make.

Periodically the firm must redetermine the appropriate salary ranges based on market and the firm's own economic factors for that year. Adjustments to the schedule may not always be possible. In that case, the market may move ahead of the firm. The past several years have forced greater changes at the lower ends of the associate compensation scale, compressing wages because increases could not be made elsewhere. While not desirable, adjustments can be driven only by market forces and the firm's ability to adjust its operations to enhance profitability.

A sample salary schedule is shown in Table 3.3. It provides for a minimum and maximum salary for each year after the second year. In the first two years, this firm has decided to operate with a lock-step system and not differentiate among its associates. Notice that the ranges overlap. That is, the maximum for one year is higher than the minimum for the next year. This is desirable in that each year does not represent discrete and isolated performance factors. This firm provides for a 10 percent differential at minimum from year to year and for a maximum that is 5 percent higher than the following year's minimum.

A firm may choose to ask an individual to leave if performance does not warrant the minimum for his or her class. That would have been the rule ten years ago. More and more firms will hold the associate back and see how performance develops. As long as the basic economics of the individual remain profitable and there is sufficient work for the firm to succeed, such a course is recommended.

TABLE 3.3 **Sample Associate Salary Schedule**

Year	*Minimum*	*Maximum*
1	$40,000	$40,000
2	$44,000	$44,000
3	$48,400	$55,900
4	$53,200	$61,400
5	$58,500	$67,600
6	$64,400	$74,300
7	$70,800	$81,800

Career Track Salary Administration

This method is very similar in operation to the years-of-experience salary administration method. The major difference is that individual years of experience are not the focal point. Rather, the firm defines a career track through which the associate may pass. The basis of such a program is to recognize that annual differences between associates are less meaningful than skill sets, that law firms must define the career track for their professional employees, and that up or out is not economically viable.

Career track programs set forth position requirements in areas that include quality and quantity of work, client relations, internal relations, personal qualities, and the like. A sample of one such program follows.

Associate (Entry Level)

Qualifications

Quality of work: Each entry-level associate is expected to be accurate, thorough, timely in work; understand the basics of areas of law; draft routine documents; and negotiate routine matters with little supervision.

Quantity of work: Each entry-level associate is expected to work a minimum of 2,000 billable hours per year. The senior attorneys and shareholders will provide sufficient files for an associate to meet this requirement.

Client relations: Each entry-level associate should be informed, reliably accurate, and diplomatic in client meetings.

Internal relations: Each entry-level associate should strive to gain the confidence of all other members of the firm.

Personal qualities: Each entry-level associate should have a strong work ethic and an ability to balance the requirements of work and personal life.

Tenure: Lawyers employed by the firm who have not yet passed the bar become entry-level associates upon licensure and are expected to require four years to develop beyond the entry level for an associate.

Compensation Potential

Entry-level associate salaries currently range from $__,000 to $__,000, *per annum*. Salary progression is based on improved performance. Adjustments to salary are made annually, effective on the employee's anniversary date of employment with the firm.

In addition to salary, associates may qualify for a bonus of up to __% of their annual salary. Bonuses are discretionary, based on both individual and firm performance and are awarded during December of each year.

Associate

Qualifications

Quality of work: Each associate should have a solid grasp of areas of law including concepts, rules, and issues; be able to draft all documents; and negotiate matters with some guidance.

Quantity of work: Each associate is expected to work 2,400 hours per year on behalf of the firm, 2,100 of which are billable and 300 of which are directed toward other firm-approved responsibilities. The senior attorneys and shareholders will provide sufficient files for an associate to meet this requirement.

Client relations: Each associate should be able to reliably counsel important clients.

Internal relations: Each associate should be helpful in serving as a resource for entry-level associates and should be able to accept direction from more senior lawyers.

New business development: Each associate should participate in community activities and develop contacts/relationships for future business development.

Personal qualities: Each associate should exhibit good people skills, have a basic sense of the profession, and function as a team player.

Tenure: Lawyers become eligible for associate status after four years from admission to the bar and one year as an entry-level associate of the firm. Associates are expected to require eight years as associates (including entry level) to qualify for promotion to senior attorney status.

Compensation Potential

Associate salaries currently range from $__,000 to $__,000, *per annum*. Salary progression is based on improved personal performance. Adjustments to salary are made annually, effective on the employee's anniversary date of employment with the firm.

In addition to salary, Associates may qualify for a bonus of up to ___% of annual salary. Bonuses are discretionary, based on both individual and firm performance and are awarded during December of each year. Associates will be paid one-third of their bonus when awarded, one-third six months after award, and one-third eighteen months after award. Deferred bonus payments require continued employment through the date of payment.

Senior Attorney

Qualifications

Quality of work: Each senior attorney should be reliable and versatile with deep expertise, enhanced by considerable experience, and have the ability to work independently with no significant professional guidance.

Quantity of work: Each senior attorney is expected to work 2,500 hours per year on behalf of the firm, 2,000 of which are client-billable and 500 of which are directed toward development of business, practice management, and business management.

Client relations: Each senior attorney should be able to reliably counsel decision-making clients, and may be the chief client contact for a specific area of law.

Internal relations: Each senior attorney should have earned and should retain the respect, trust, and confidence of partners, peers, and other personnel.

New business development: Senior attorneys are expected to have more than enough client relationships to provide sufficient work for themselves and others.

Personal qualities: Each senior attorney should have the judgment and maturity to handle most major problems without supervision, and enhanced people skills in team problem-solving situations and client development/relations.

Tenure: Lawyers become eligible for senior attorney status after eight years from admission to the bar and two years as an associate of the firm. Senior attorneys are expected to spend at least three years as senior attorneys of the firm to qualify for promotion to shareholder status. The firm does not have an "up or out" policy, and therefore progression to shareholder status may or may not occur.

Compensation Potential

Senior attorney salaries currently range from $___,000 to $___,000, *per annum*. Salary progression is based on improved performance. Adjustments to salary are made annually, effective on the employee's anniversary date of employment with the firm.

In addition to salary, senior attorneys may qualify for a bonus of up to ___% of annual salary. Bonuses are based on individual, team, and firm performance. Bonuses are awarded during December of each year. Senior attorneys will be paid one-third of their bonus when awarded, one-third six months after award, and one-third eighteen months after award. Deferred bonus payments require continued employment through the date of payment. Deferred bonus payments will be made if termination of employment is due to death or permanent disability.

Shareholder

Qualification

Quality of work: Shareholders are expected to have achieved excellence in legal scholarship, expertise in broad practice areas, and be capable of solving complex problems.

Quantity of work: Each shareholder should commit 2,500 hours to the benefit of the firm, 1,900 of which are billable and 600 of which are devoted to the management of the practice and the firm and the development of business.

Client relations: Shareholders should counsel executive-level clients and nurture client relationships at a very high level.

Internal relations: Shareholders must collaborate with each other and with other personnel, cooperate and support the common effort, effectively train and teach younger lawyers, and demonstrate a true spirit of partnership.

New business development: Shareholders must be able to manage client relationships, and bring new clients and business into the firm, providing work not only for themselves, but also for others.

Personal qualities: Shareholders must be stable, mature, decisive, and exhibit superior judgment.

Compensation Potential

Shareholder draws currently begin at $___,000, *per annum*. Bonuses may be awarded.

Individual Performance Salary Administration

This salary administration system is probably the most difficult program to design because of its lack of structure. Salary and bonus are no longer separate concepts. Compensation in such firms can approach almost a commission orientation where the associate is paid a low salary plus a percentage of fees collected and business produced. The percentages may range from as low as 10 percent to as high as 50 percent. Smaller law firms are more likely to have such systems, as are plaintiff personal injury practices. There are often several reasons why this arrangement is undesirable from the point of view of the employer.

First, the clients that most young associates can obtain are those that do not pay well. Because they are paid a salary to work on these matters and receive a percentage of the gross as well, the economics of this system do not affect the associate, but they may adversely affect the employer. Using our earlier example, the firm cannot afford much of a commission without subsidizing the program. Most firms do not adjust the salary low enough to make such a proposition reasonable; therefore, they find themselves in the position of passing profits back down to the associates.

Second, when an associate receives premiums or commissions for bringing in a client, priority will be given to those personal clients rather than to clients of the firm. This defeats the original purpose of hiring an associate, which almost invariably is because the firm has more work than it can handle. It also diverts productive energies of the associates from the generally more established, more lucrative clients of the firm toward work of lesser quality.

Such arrangements are, therefore, often undesirable because of the little regard for the profitability of the work, the overhead required, or the desirability of such work for the firm.

However, there are reasons to consider individually based performance salary plans. The firm can adopt a plan that progresses an individual along a salary path that rewards established economic and client service performance. This can be done using either the years-of-experience or career track salary administration method.

BONUSES

Most law firms pay performance-based bonuses. Smaller law firms are more likely to provide for such payments; however, they are quite common at larger firms. Although most firms profess that their bonus structure is discretionary, the author's experience is that in operation, many of these plans are quite inflexible. In fact, they are viewed by most associates as a lump-sum salary payment that is deferred to year-end.

Those firms may have structured a low base salary and compensate that with consistently high year-end bonuses. Such a strategy is not recommended as it may place the firm at a perceived competitive disadvantage. Most young lawyers compare salaries, not total earnings, when they get together to compare firms. Consequently, those firms that operate with such a system may reap competitive benefits by eliminating the bonus and raising salaries. Higher base pay may also be more highly valued by the associates, such that a $20,000 year-end bonus may be worth $15,000 in additional salary.

On the other hand, a discretionary bonus arrangement can provide a control mechanism over labor costs and allow for immediate outstanding performance recognition. Fees generated, clients produced, and other factors are consistently weighed by law firms in developing bonuses. However, only a few firms really reward only the extraordinary individual performance or superlative firm achievement. In fact, bonuses often are paid to nearly every associate in the firm.

One common incentive is the production-based bonus. When an associate can get a percentage of gross production over some minimum threshold there is an incentive to work hard. If the incentive is based on fees collected or billings, it prevents the associate from overworking files, but places the individual at the mercy of the billing partner who, if not constrained, may simply allocate all negative adjustments to the associate, regardless of merit. If the incentive is based on hours, there is the problem of overworking files to the detriment of the client. Carefully drafted rules for adjustments and enforcement of the rules set forth are necessary for effective operation of such systems. The authors recommend that the partners, not the associates, absorb the discount or premium of billing adjustments. At least, the adjustments should be allocated based on relative time value among all timekeepers on the matter.

Another incentive system combines individual and firm performance factors with a numeric scoring system to reward associates. One such plan is discussed below.

Associate Compensation Program

Salary

Salary is established based on market conditions, performance, service to the firm over time, years of experience, training, and day-to-day responsibilities. Different salary ranges exist for various levels of professional staff at the firm.

Associate	$___,000 to $___,000
Senior Associate	$___,000 to $___,000
Principal	$___,000 to $___,000

Bonus Program

Philosophy. The bonus program provides the potential to earn additional compensation based on both individual and firm performance. The firm will consider factors that cannot be readily measured in awarding bonus money. Such factors include efforts, assignment responsibilities for management, training, and the like. However, the attorneys must recognize that the primary criterion is the rendering of quality, timely, and cost-effective legal services on behalf of clients that are important to the short- and long-term success of the firm. These services must be of superior value and integrity and must be performed in an efficient manner, measured not just against alternatives, but also in absolute terms. While recognizing that the ideal is never achievable, the firm acknowledges that nothing less can be an acceptable goal. The foregoing must take place within an environment that permits high levels of personal satisfaction and achievement by all attorneys.

Objectives. The incentive compensation system for the firm should drive the organization toward four basic objectives:

1. Encourage excellence in client service;
2. Encourage teamwork;
3. Encourage productivity; and
4. Retain talented employees.

Each objective will facilitate achievement of the firm's goals. Following is a brief rationale for each objective.

- *Encourage excellence in client service*—Clients are the lifeblood of the business of law. Each member of the firm must know the firm's clients, understand their needs, and work diligently on their behalf.

- *Encourage teamwork*—The practice of law today is a complex endeavor that requires interdisciplinary efforts and coordination among lawyers, legal assistants, and administrative and support staff. Teamwork must be demonstrated among the members of the firm. It must be clear that the success of the individual is dependent upon the success of the firm as a whole.
- *Encourage productivity*—It is imperative that the resources of the firm are put to their highest and best use. Review of firm processes must occur with the objective of improving and streamlining those processes to ensure the most timely and cost-effective delivery of legal services possible. Efficiencies will ensure that: (1) each employee's skills are utilized; (2) responsiveness is as rapid as possible; (3) duplication of effort is eliminated; (4) automation is used to enhance productivity; and (5) redundant and unnecessary work is eliminated.
- *Retain talented employees*—There is a significant cost associated with underutilized and discouraged employees: the loss of talented employees, and the need to replace their talents and knowledge of the law. It is incumbent upon the firm to ensure that employees are well treated and compensated appropriately and competitively. Implementation of a firm bonus program will assist in that objective.

Eligibility. The incentive plan will be prorated on an annual basis, and all attorneys will be eligible with the following stipulations:

- Each new employee must have a minimum of six months of service.
- Employees who retire or are ill during the calendar year will be eligible for the incentive plan on a prorated basis.

Bonus pool. The firm shall establish a bonus savings fund in which it will deposit funds throughout the year. The size of the pool will likely change from year to year. Attorneys shall be kept informed as to the size of the bonus fund.

Criteria.

- *Fee production*—Fees produced, measured at the time of collection (cash receipts), will be valued based on individual performance as a working attorney and for the firm overall. The firm's goal will be measured on an average per full-time equivalent attorney basis. Each lawyer shall have a goal for fee production for purposes of establishing the firm target.

Individual fee production compared to individual goal	***Individual points***
greater than 20% unfavorable variance	0.00
10% unfavorable variance to 20% unfavorable variance	0.50
10% unfavorable variance to firm target	1.50
Firm target to 10% favorable variance	2.50
10% favorable variance to 20% favorable variance	5.00
greater than 20% favorable variance	8.00

- *Average profitability per file*—Measured as the ratio of net fees produced (total paid to firm less direct costs of file as determined by firm's cost allocation system) to total paid to firm. Each attorney and the firm's overall performance will be evaluated. The firm's goal will be based on a three-year historical average. Individuals will be evaluated against the firm goal. Individual points will based on an overall average for the year.

Individual file profitability ratio compared to firm goal	***Individual points***
greater than 20% unfavorable variance	0.00
10% unfavorable variance to 20% unfavorable variance	0.25
10% unfavorable variance to firm target	0.75
Firm target to 10% favorable variance	1.25
10% favorable variance to 20% favorable variance	2.50
greater than 20% favorable variance	4.00

- *Average turnaround per file*—Measured in months from the date the file is received in office until client receives settlement or the matter is closed. Each attorney and the firm's overall performance will be evaluated. The firm's goal will be based on a three-year historical average. Individuals will be evaluated against the firm goal.

Individual average turnaround in months compared to firm goal	***Individual points***
greater than 10% unfavorable variance	0.00
10% unfavorable variance to firm target	0.25
Firm target to 10% favorable variance	0.50
10% favorable variance to 20% favorable variance	1.20
greater than 20% favorable variance	2.40

- *Subjective determination*—Established by the firm based on a determination of effort, other accomplishments, seniority, and other factors deemed relevant. The firm can award anywhere from 0 to 1.6 points. Normal award would be .75 points.

Calculation and weighting. Bonuses will be calculated by assigning points to each of the criteria. For each criteria, firm performance will affect the final points an individual will accumulate.

Firm performance compared to target	*Firm factor*
greater than 20% unfavorable variance	0.00
10% unfavorable variance to 20% unfavorable variance	0.25
10% unfavorable variance to firm target	0.75
Firm target to 10% favorable variance	1.00
10% favorable variance to 20% favorable variance	1.10
greater than 20% favorable variance	1.25

Employee Points = Fee production points + File profitability points + Average turnaround points + Subjective points.

Weighted Firm Factor = [.60 x Firm fee production factor] + [.30 x Firm file profitability factor] x [.10 x Firm file turnaround factor].

Bonus = Employee Salary x Employee Points % x Weighted Firm Factor.

Under this plan, the maximum bonus would be 20 percent. This would require the highest individual and firm ratings for each criteria. Normal bonus under this plan, which assumes performance at target for individuals and firm, would be 5 percent.

Example. John: $75,000 salary

John is at target on fee production, 10 percent below target for file productivity, and 20 percent favorable compared to file turnaround.

The firm is 20 percent above target on fee production, at target for file profitability, and 25 percent unfavorable for file turnaround.

The firm awards John 1.6 subjective points for practice management and associate training efforts.

John's bonus:

Employee points	= 2.50 + 0.75 + 2.40 + 1.60
	= 7.25
Firm factor	= (0.60 x 1.25) + (0.30 x 1.00) + (0.10 x 0.00)
	= 0.75 + 0.30 + 0.00
	= 1.05
Bonus	= $75,000 x 7.25% x 1.05
	= $5,709

The key to successful implementation of an incentive program such as the one just described is to select only three or four critical factors to measure. At least one factor should be subjectively awarded to balance objective criteria.

Production-based incentives are often paid monthly or quarterly. While this incentive rewards the individual almost immediately, it can create problems for the employer. First, there is the potential for manipulation of work to boost period performance and achieve or increase the bonus. The consequence is that the following period's performance may not meet expectations. Adjustments or subsidiary bookkeeping can mitigate this, but with additional administrative burden.

Second, paying bonuses periodically under such a scheme results in additional payroll complexities. Ideally, the payroll should be a nonevent once it is set up at the beginning of the year.

Bonuses can be just as rewarding when paid at year-end, with less bookkeeping and payroll disruption.

CHAPTER 4

Paraprofessional Compensation

OVERVIEW

The attributes of compensating paralegal assistants are similar to that of associate lawyers described earlier. Paralegal compensation systems are often aligned with those of associates, only the dollars involved are less.

The most significant issue regarding paralegal compensation is whether the individual is "exempt" or "nonexempt" under the wage and hour laws (Fair Labor Standards Act—FLSA). Unfortunately, there is no clear answer. It will depend on the facts and circumstances of the positions within your firm. In fact, you may have both exempt and nonexempt paralegal assistant positions within your firm. This is, however, an important issue, as it affects the payment of overtime compensation. Appendix 4 sets forth the general specification regarding exemption. The following guidelines are to provide assistance with respect to paralegals. They are not determinative. Each firm will need to conduct an appropriate review of case and statutory law. Expert assistance is recommended.

PARALEGAL CLASSIFICATIONS

Paralegal assistants may qualify for an exempt position as either a professional or administrative employee. Let's review each classification.

- *Professional*—The most difficult test is whether the position's primary duties require advanced knowledge customarily acquired through advanced instruction. It has been the author's experience that other similar positions have not met this test even though they require extensive educational training. To compound the difficulty, only 20 percent of the individual's time can be devoted to "nonprofessional" duties. Given this narrow definition and interpretation it may be unlikely that a paralegal position would be granted an exemption as a professional employee.

- *Administrative*—The requirements for primary job duties are office and nonmanual work relating to management and operations of the employer. Further, they must customarily exercise discretion and independent judgment, require only general supervision, assist an executive, and perform job duties requiring special skills. These definitions could be satisfied by many paralegals. The other requirements for nonexempt work and salary will most likely be met, but cannot be overlooked.

Each firm must decide for itself if each position is qualified for an exemption and whether the firm wants to face the possibility of justifying its position. Page & Addison, P.C., a small Dallas, Texas, law firm, was successful in defending its paralegals as exempt as administrative employees in a Department of Labor suit. (*U.S. Department of Labor vs. Page & Addison, P.C.*, U.S. District Court, Dallas, No. 91-2655). A March 16, 1994, *Wall Street Journal* article nicely summarized the varied issues and interests in the classification of paralegals as exempt or nonexempt.

PARALEGAL COMPENSATION

Because paralegals are fee producers, their compensation can be based on the production of fee revenues. In evaluating paralegals, firms must be comfortable using fee earner data. That is, a standard means of allocating overhead among all fee earners (partners, associates, and paralegals). The generally accepted standard is that one lawyer equals two paralegal assistants equals one fee earner. Therefore, a law firm with ten lawyers and five paralegal assistants has 12.5 fee earners. This is the standard definition used in most surveys. Table 4.1 depicts an average paralegal. As you can see, *at the average*, paralegals are not profitable. This, of course, does not consider nonbillable or nonchargeable contributions that are a significant portion of many paralegals' duties. Those firms who utilize paralegals efficiently have found them to be productive and profitable contributors.

Individual firms may develop other means of allocation. The authors have seen rational systems that treat a paralegal from one-quarter to three-fourths of a fee earner. Some firms even allocate differently among the lawyers. Each firm must look to its own data and use of resources balanced against some measure of simplicity and ease of calculation.

TABLE 4.1 **Profitability of Paralegals**

	Paralegals as a Group	Paralegals as a Percent of Associates
Fee production		
Average annual billable hours	$1,411	77.4%
Average standard billing rate	61	50.4%
Fee production	86,071	39.0%
Average time written off	(7,176)	39.0%
Billable fees produced	78,895	39.0%
Position costs		
Average overhead	43,820	50.0%
Average total compensation	37,670	50.7%
Position cost	81,490	50.3%
Profitability		
Cash basis profit (Loss)	(2,595)	
Cash basis margin	(3.0%)	

Source: *1994 Altman Weil Pensa Survey of Law Firm Economics*, Altman Weil Pensa Publications, Inc., Newtown Square, PA 19073.

Paralegal compensation can then be structured much like that of the associates. It is preferable to establish a uniform compensation philosophy that is consistent across all employees. This simplifies administrative aspects and sends a consistent message to every fee producer regarding the activities that are important to success.

Unfortunately, as can be seen from the above example, paralegal utilization is less than 80 percent of the average associate. The reasons for this are many and varied. It is in the economic interests of clients, the firm, and the paralegals to improve utilization.

Because the utilization of such individuals lags and is often outside of the control of the individual, compensation structures must not penalize the individual for results that are failings of the system or the firm and not that of the individual. Paralegal time is often hit the hardest when write-offs are taken on a matter. They are the lowest rung on the fee producer ladder with far more limited career opportunities than the lawyers. The rationale often goes like this: "It won't hurt their careers or their income." That attitude may prevail even in a firm that pays paralegals bonuses based on fee generation.

However, many paralegals may not be hired primarily for billable work. In those instances their compensation structure must reflect the relative value of the position. See Chapter 5 for a discussion of such systems.

It is, therefore, important to establish an appropriate psychological environment among all fee producers so that personal income opportunities are not artificially diminished. This extends beyond billing to staffing and task assignments.

It may be appropriate in certain situations to grant fictitious fee credits for continuing legal education, accounting tasks, bar activities, *pro bono* work, and the like. Such assignments may be more cost-effective for the firm if handled by paralegals. Accordingly, compensation should recognize such value.

If you have paralegals assigned to high-risk or contingent matters, then they should share in the allocation of premiums to compensate for their work on those matters where no fee is earned.

Paralegal compensation varies by location, size of firm, and other factors. Table 4.2 provides a sample of such variability.

TABLE 4.2 **Selected Paralegal Compensation Data**[1]

	Lower Quartile (Paralegal)	*Ninth Decile (Paralegal Supervisor)*
West	$29,421	$57,805
Northeast	24,746	63,878
Under 9 Lawyers	22,000	57,640
Over 75 Lawyers	26,249	54,818
Under 100,000 population	22,214	47,591
Over 1,000,000 population	28,676	60,910

[1]W-2 plus employers paid benefits and payroll taxes.

Source: *1994 Altman Weil Pensa Survey of Law Firm Economics*, Altman Weil Pensa Publications, Inc., Newtown Square, PA 19073.

CHAPTER 5
Staff Compensation

OVERVIEW

As law firms have grown in the number of lawyers they employ, so has the number of staff structures that support them. Law firm support staffs used to be small and consist predominately of hourly employees. Such individuals were primarily concerned with their hourly rate or weekly take-home pay. Little sophistication was required in administration of their compensation structure.

Larger firms today employ a significant number of semi-professional and managerial employees who are not covered by the overtime requirements of the labor laws. These employees need salary and benefit packages that differ from those offered to hourly employees. While much of the "structuring" is the same, such positions tend to have increased benefit packages and bonus structures that are tied to group performance.

The nonlawyer staff is generally covered by the provisions of the Fair Labor Standards Act (FLSA). That means that the employer must meet minimum wage standards and must comply with the overtime pay provisions of that act. Only employees with real managerial and supervisory duties are generally excluded from FLSA coverage; these may include, for example, the legal administrator, an office manager with real authority, a paralegal supervisor, or a recruiter. See Appendix 4 for a summary of the exemptions to the overtime requirements of the FLSA.

NONEXEMPT STAFF

Personnel policies for the nonexempt staff of the law office must be based on consideration of the reasons this group of people works. The objectives and motivation of staff are somewhat different from those of lawyers. Consider these factors:

- Many staff employees are secondary wage earners. That is, they work to supplement family income. However, some find that they become the primary wage earner because of a divorce, a nonworking spouse, or for other reasons.
- Many employees have primary parental responsibilities for children and may have elder-care responsibilities as well.

- These occupations have a shorter training period than a profession, and also have a shorter on-the-job learning curve.
- There are few opportunities for advancement on the staff of a law office. While an associate lawyer may have a goal of becoming a partner, a secretary has little to achieve by way of advancement. Immediate reward is, therefore, more important.
- An important part of compensation is psychological rather than monetary. Being useful, needed, and appreciated are important to staff (although these factors are not discussed here).

Staff is generally hired in a local labor market. A messenger or secretary will rarely travel more than a few miles to a job and is unlikely to relocate to obtain a new one. Consequently, the prevailing wage patterns that are important in fixing and comparing salary scales are those in the immediate locality. Because staff personnel can generally move between industries, wage patterns in all types of offices are pertinent to the compensation scale of the staff of a law office. There are a number of sources of local wage information. In many cities, private employer groups collect and disseminate such data. Check with the local Chamber of Commerce, State Employment Service, and the local Association of Legal Administrators chapter to determine if they know of such sources. There are two national sources of local wage data, available for many cities and some regions:

1. The United States Department of Labor, Bureau of Labor Statistics, conducts metropolitan area studies that generally contain information, by industry and size of employer, on office pay. (See Appendix 5.)
2. The Association of Legal Administrators (175 E. Hawthorn Parkway, Suite 325, Vernon Hills, IL 60061-1428; 708-816-1212), conducts surveys of the compensation of nineteen nonlawyer administrative positions. Information is provided by region, state, metropolitan area, length of experience, level of education, level of supervisory responsibility, and by size of law firm. Data for means, medians, and 1st and 3rd quartiles are provided where possible. Each position is defined in the introduction. (See the tables in Appendix 5.)

Setting Wage Scales

Every job has a minimum value. You just can't find people with the necessary skills to take the job and stay for any length of time for less than that. If you refer to local surveys, the first quartile amount (25th percentile) will generally be near the minimum you would pay in a law office. The lowest paid quarter of employees are not likely to meet law office standards of skill and performance.

The third quartile (75th percentile) of wages in the local market may be about your upper limit, except for a few employees. Every job has a maximum worth. To illustrate, a secretary is usually paid less than a lawyer—even a young lawyer in today's market. Also, a good legal secretary is generally paid more than a receptionist or a messenger. This natural hierarchy of jobs sets upper limits, as does the employer's desire to limit labor costs.

The tables from the Bureau of Labor Statistics found in Appendix 5 show the salary ranges of a number of jobs. These charts illustrate the idea of minimum and maximum worth.

There is another simple way to order the staff pay scale to help set a minimum and maximum value on jobs and to determine the number of years it should take to advance through the scale. That is to examine two factors: (1) the number of years it will take to reach maximum efficiency in a job, and (2) the disruption value of having to find and train a replacement. The second factor could be expressed as the equivalent of a number (or fraction) of years. Some jobs are related. For example, it is common to group secretarial jobs in a separate hierarchy, starting perhaps with transcription typist, then junior secretary, and finally senior secretary. The content of these related jobs will increase because of the work performed by the principals to whom the position relates.

Table 5.1 shows a listing of common law firm staff positions with possible year values assigned.

TABLE 5.1 **A Law Office Job Listing**

	Years Required for		
	Maximum Performance	*Replacement Value*	*Total Years to Maximum Value*
Messenger	1		1
Copy machine operator	1	0	1
Filing assistant	2	0.5	2.5
Telephone operator	2	0.5	2.5
Receptionist	2	1	3
Data entry clerk	2	0.5	2.5
Secretarial group (cumulative)			
Transcription typist[1]	2	0.5	2.5
Word processor operator I[1]	3	1	4
Junior secretary[2]	4	1.5	5.5
Word processor operator II	4	2	6
Senior secretary	4	2	6
Bookkeeper (full charge)	8	2	10

[1]Count cumulatively toward senior secretary or WP operator II.
[2]Count cumulatively toward senior secretary.

The number of years normally needed to become proficient in an office job can be estimated. The disruption value is more arbitrary, and each office can set its own numbers. If a job has a learning period of two years and a disruption value of one year, then an incumbent should be able to progress from the minimum pay for the job to the maximum in the total period, or three years.

There are elaborate systems for rationalizing the pay scale. For office clerical jobs, however, a simple ranking system usually suffices. In such a system, one creates a hierarchy of jobs by looking at the traditional relative values of them, by obtaining wage statistics like those in the Bureau of Labor Statistics chart, and then creating job classes.

Here's what the job classification plan of a law firm with a full range of office jobs might look like. First, we will arbitrarily place each of the identified separate jobs in a salary grade:

Messenger	Grade 1
Copy machine operator	Grade 1
Filing assistant	Grade 2
Telephone operator	Grade 2
Receptionist	Grade 3
Data entry clerk	Grade 2
Transcription typist	Grade 2
Word processing operator I	Grade 3
Junior secretary	Grade 3
Word processing operator II	Grade 5
Senior secretary	Grade 5
Bookkeeper, full charge	Grade 8

Each grade is then assigned a range of points, depending on its level of difficulty and the job market. Simple, hourly jobs have a small range. The top is reached after one or two years. Highly skilled or managerial jobs have a much larger range, with the maximum to be reached over a longer period of time. In larger organizations with complex job structures, the assignment of point values to job grades is usually accomplished through formal salary administration/evaluation plans. In law firms, with their small number of different jobs, a simple ranking system such as the one illustrated is enough to place positions into an order, and the use of comparative labor market information coupled with individual employee performance can be used to create rate ranges and individual salaries.

It is useful to assign a point range to each job grade so that the relative positions of the grades are not affected by inflation of the wage scale. With a point system, it is only necessary to assign a dollar value to each point to translate points to salary (See Ill 5.1).

ILL 5.1 **A Job Hierarchy**

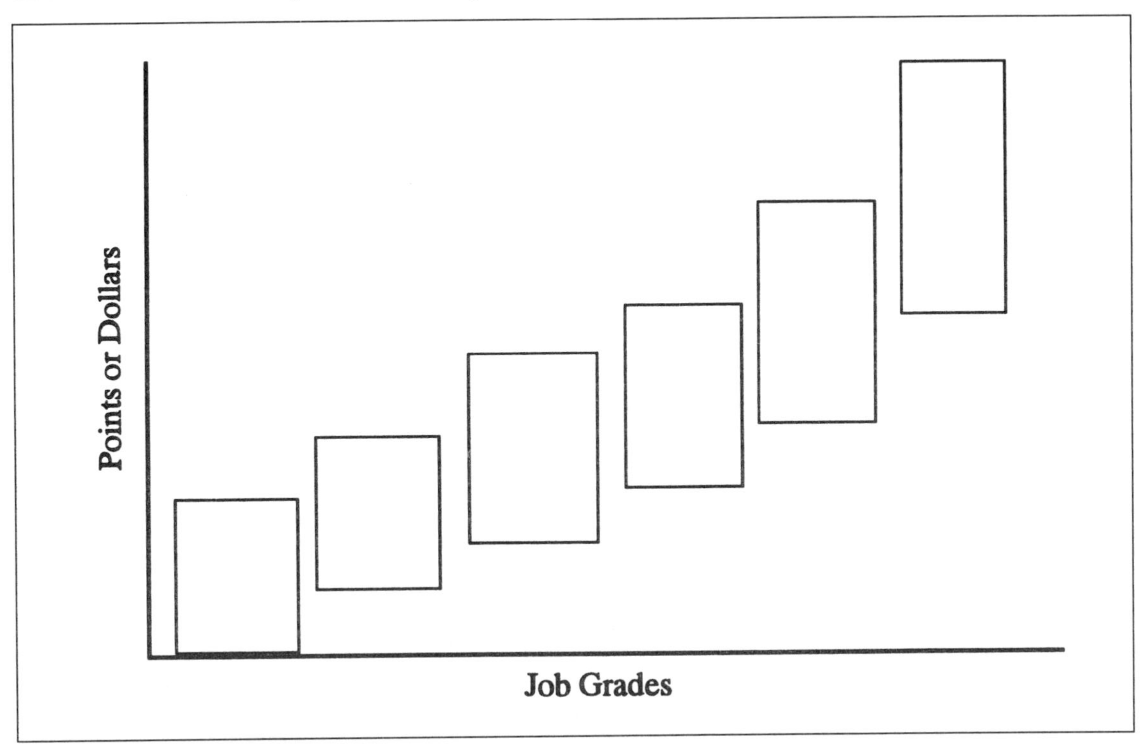

Salary Increases

Salary review, especially in smaller law offices, has many political facets. Lawyers may want to procure an increase for their personal secretaries to ensure that they receive maximum support or to assuage their own egos. The result may be interpartner warfare and compensation of staff, based on boss power rather than value to the firm or equity.

Any system designed to compensate people can be subject to abuse, of course, even when administered centrally through a personnel committee or an office administrator rather than by the dictates of individual partners. But in general, when one permits one manager or a small committee to undertake a salary review and then to determine advances, there is a better chance that the process will be impartial and benefit both employer and employees.

In small law firms, the process of handing out raises will generally be (and should be) relatively informal. There may be no need to do more than carefully consider each employee's contributions, and deal with the topic once a year. However, the results must be fully and carefully communicated to individual employees, even when the determination is made informally.

Larger organizations (those with twenty or more staff employees) will need a more formal evaluation program. This is because an individual manager or a small committee will not be able to judge the performance and value of a large number of people without the benefit of a system. In larger firms, the development of detailed, specific procedures and the implementation of an evaluation system can most effectively be handled by a trained, experienced personnel or office manager.

Through the performance appraisal process, each employee should know what is expected of him or her in the performance of the job. The best way to develop an understanding of these expectations between a firm and its employees is through the use of detailed job descriptions. Each description should state the job title, the person(s) to whom the employee reports, a general description of job functions (for example: "a word processing operator is responsible for the production and revision of standard legal documents on word processing equipment as assigned"), and a complete description of all job duties. A secretary is not merely expected to do typing, but is expected to "type in a timely fashion, with a minimum of errors, all letters, memos, briefs, forms, and other documents as requested by assigned attorneys. Such typing is to be performed at a designated work station using equipment and supplies provided by the firm." Employees should also understand what is expected regarding attendance, overtime work, willingness to assist other employees who may be overburdened, and other matters. Many law office jobs can be reduced to written job descriptions. Support staff employees should be encouraged to review their job descriptions once a year, with attorney/supervisor review, and these may be used by reviewers in the evaluation process.

Informal performance appraisal should take place on a continuing basis. There should be frequent communication between employee and supervisor regarding job performance. If daily review occurs, employees will generally not be surprised when formal evaluations are delivered.

Here are some guidelines for supervisors in conducting evaluation discussions with employees:

- Allow enough time to have a full discussion without interruption.
- Reduce tension by encouraging the employee to sit comfortably in your office.
- Maintain eye contact and listen carefully to be sure that the employee understands.
- Focus on proficiencies and deficiencies in the performance of the job, not on personality traits.
- Be sure to include strengths, as well as weaknesses, in your discussion, but do not give the wrong impression if the overall rating is unsatisfactory.
- Encourage a discussion of how the employee can improve performance. Emphasize the future.

- Be prepared to acknowledge disagreements, but ensure that the employee understands that the firm expects him or her to perform according to certain standards.

Review procedures should be incorporated into the firm's office manual. These procedures should be discussed with new employees at initial orientation sessions. This process will ensure that new employees understand the firm's evaluation process and salary program, and the reasons for them, and that the evaluation will aid the employee in his or her work.

Most firms should review employees initially after three to six months of employment, and thereafter on their anniversary dates of employment. This makes it possible for evaluations to occur throughout the year, thus relieving the pressure to do all reviews at once. Salary adjustments, however, should generally be made once each year, based on each employee's most recent review, budgetary guidelines established by the firm, and inflation pressures. Many employers will make a 5 percent adjustment if the employee successfully completes the initial three-to-six-month probationary period.

The performance review should match the expectations communicated to the employee at the start of employment. Job descriptions should be reviewed, discussed, and modified as appropriate. Standard forms are other tools of the evaluation process.

The office or personnel manager is usually responsible for ensuring that performance evaluations occur. The manager should remind lawyers and supervisors to complete evaluation forms at anniversary dates and be sure that the process is completed shortly thereafter. The office or personnel manager is usually responsible for the central collection of employment records on firm personnel, including evaluation forms.

In many law offices, it is not appropriate for only the employee's immediate supervisor to complete evaluation forms. Typically, the attorneys work together on projects, and the secretaries help one another to get the work done. Thus, attorneys will have contact with several secretaries and will be able to participate in the evaluation process for each of them. There is often less crossover of work among support groups such as messengers and word processing, so their only evaluators may be support department supervisors.

It is the responsibility of the office or personnel manager to determine the personnel involved in each of the firm's various groups, to contact all appropriate raters at anniversary dates, and to collect evaluation forms from all raters. The manager should review each form to ensure that a fair, objective evaluation has been given. Attorneys and other supervisors who are deficient or ineffective in giving written employee evaluations should be counseled. After all forms have been completed and reviewed, the office or personnel manager or supervisor should conduct a private evaluation conference with each rated employee.

Through other administrative systems, employers should collect separate, objective records on each employee's performance. For example, sign-in/sign-out sheets and time records can be used to monitor employee attendance; telephone and photocopy charge slips can be reviewed to ensure that they are completed; and the clerical supervisor can comment on the cooperation of secretaries in accepting overflow work. In word processing, production records may be considered.

EXEMPT STAFF

Managerial, technical, and professional positions are treated separately from office and clerical positions. Some of this distinction arises from different treatment under the FLSA. Other differences arise from the educational backgrounds required, the length of time it takes to become proficient, the general level of supervision required, and the like. Unfortunately, many law firms have not fully integrated their burgeoning middle management into their overall job value system. They have recognized that these individuals fall somewhere in between the office staff and the lawyers.

Senior Management

Providing some structure to senior management positions begins by first segregating senior management from middle management. Senior management is characterized by the closeness with which they work with the owners. These individuals immerse themselves into the position in such a way that it can be difficult to separate the person from the position. Senior management deals with stewardship of the owners' interests (which, at least in the District of Columbia, may include their own interests) and strategic decisions as opposed to operational decisions. It is characteristic of this position to have mostly exempt middle managers reporting to it. Performance measurements tend to be structured around overall firm performance (i.e., growth in partner income) and control and efficiency of non-legal operations (overhead per fee earner, staffing ratios, satisfaction surveys, and the like).

At this level, age and length of service tend to have very little correlation with compensation. However, the organization's size is very much considered. Very small law firms may consider these functions as a responsibility of each partner, operating as a committee of the whole. As firms grow, they may assign these functions to a managing partner or to an executive committee. Only in the larger law firms do separate senior nonlawyer executives exist. Note that the office managers in many firms do not function at this level even though they may be the highest compensated nonlawyer administrative employees in the firm.

The labor market for senior management is certainly national in scope. National wage data are critical to determining the prevailing levels of compensation. However, in law firms there is an executive compensation flash point. Unlike publicly traded companies where executives can earn nearly unlimited sums of money if performance warrants (we will not debate whether such compensation plans really do pay for performance in this text), executives in law firms face a compensation ceiling of average partner compensation levels. It would be rare indeed to find a nonlawyer CEO of a law firm earning consistently higher than the average partner in his or her firm. Accordingly, it is less likely that there will be a formal salary range for the position.

Middle Management

Middle management is a class of worker very much in transition. The last recession brought to the United States its first decrease in white collar employment. Unlike earlier blue collar recessions, most of these jobs were not temporary layoffs, they were major restructurings that eliminated the positions altogether. Certainly, in every industry, there is a critical eye cast regarding the need for and actual contributions of middle management. Organizations are becoming flatter, bringing the front line workers closer to decision makers, bypassing the need for decision coordinators (middle management).

Middle management positions must be evaluated in this context. Are they critical to the delivery of legal services and the servicing of clients' needs? Law firms will find that many of these positions are not. Those who remain will be multi-skilled, well informed about the organization and its operations, flexible in job function, and creative in job process.

It will be these factors that will govern performance evaluation as we approach the end of this century. Salaries will be set by regional and possibly national markets. Salary ranges exist and can be coordinated with the overall pay scales of the organization. Increases that used to revolve around past pay, internal/external equity, consistent movement (seniority), potential, and performance, will now be made based on productivity and contribution to the firm's mission. Perhaps the best conceptualization is to instill a sense that the firm is a client of the middle manager, not just an employer.

Supervisors

This is the lowest level of the exempt group or the highest level of the nonexempt group. Pay considerations are usually strongly correlated with that of the subordinates supervised. These positions are often problematic in that they rarely contribute directly to the profits (a fact well known by the supervisors). Another problem is that the position cannot control much of the outcome of the subordinates, efforts. The training ground for supervisors is the subordinate positions they supervise.

These positions will be defined and assigned pay levels in the very traditional manner of the office positions discussed earlier. They share the same local market, and in most firms, will represent an internal promotion for an existing subordinate.

CONCLUSION

Paying staff the right amount and communicating pay decisions properly require care and planning. Lawyers who don't think through the process may pay too little—which can result in the loss of valuable people. Or they may pay too much and earn less themselves. Those law offices that are fortunate enough to have competent administrators generally rely upon them to provide a professional salary administration program.

APPENDIX I

One Firm's Rules for Allocation of Client Production Credit*

Underlying Premises

1. The long-followed concept that remuneration should be provided for the function of causing clients to patronize the firm is sound, fair, and should be continued.
2. The total amount of such remuneration is not dealt with herein. See firm's "Income Division Plan."
3. Basic to various of the firm's policies and practices are the concepts that no client is an individual firm member's client, but every client is the firm's client, and that, as between the firm and a client, all work performed for the client is performed by the firm and not by one or more particular firm members. It is, therefore, logical that to the extent that work performed for one client results in the engagement of the firm by another client who is not a "related client" (hereinafter defined), the new client ought to be deemed to have been originated at least in part by the partners.
4. When a new client comes to the firm not because of a connection with one or more particular firm members, and his advent is not known to be related to the firm's work for a prior client or some other similar factor, all of the past practice of the partners as a group ought to be deemed to be the cause of the advent of such new client.
5. After a number of years of regular repeated service to a client, responsibility for such client's continuing to patronize the firm becomes blurred. In such case, it is logical to reward the income-sharing firm members (as a group) with part of the originators' share of the fees paid by such clients, on the theory that their work in prior years is in substantial measure responsible for the continued patronage.
6. Any scheme of income division ought to furnish a financial incentive to each firm member to try to see to it that each client's work is performed by whichever firm members can, all things considered, most efficiently perform it. Accordingly, and as a limitation on paragraph 5, above, the initial originators of a client should always con-

*This document illustrates the complexity of the subject and the number of issues involved.

tinue to receive a portion of the originators' share of the fees paid by such client, subject to the consideration that it is impractical to account for minor fractions of a share.

Rules

Part A. *General Rules.* Every firm member who has a substantial known connection with the advent of a new client shall be entitled to an aliquot part of the total originating credits provided in the firm's Income Division Plan for fees paid by such new client. If one or more firm members and the firm have a substantial connection with the advent of a new client, each such firm member and the partners as a group, shall be entitled to an aliquot part of the aforesaid originating credits. If no firm member is known to have a substantial connection with the advent of a new client, the partners as a group shall be entitled to all of the aforesaid originating credits.

Rule A-1. *Definition of Firm Members.* "Firm member," as used in these rules, encompasses those persons who are partners or associates of the firm.

Rule A-2. *Division of Originating Credits Among Partners.* Originating credits allocable to partners as a group shall be divided among the individual partners as is provided in the firm's Income Division Plan.

Rule A-3. *Definition of New Client.* "New client," as used in these rules, will, absent compelling reasons otherwise, be deemed to encompass not only the individual who contacts a firm member for legal services, but all other individuals with like interests that the firm comes to represent with respect to the legal matter for which services are first sought by such individual. When it clearly appears that a former client for whom legal services have not been performed for a substantial period of time comes to a firm member for new legal services for reasons clearly unrelated to the prior representation or work associations with firm members, the client shall be deemed a new client.

Part B. *Rules Applicable to Work-Oriented, Referral-Oriented, and Supplier-Oriented New Clients.* The rules of this part B rather than the rules of part A, above, shall determine who is entitled to receive the originating credits for work-oriented, referral-oriented, and supplier-oriented new clients.

Rule B-1. *Work-Oriented New Clients.* A work-oriented new client is either: (1) one who initially became acquainted with the firm or a firm member by being directly exposed to prior work performed by the firm for another client or other clients, or (2) one who is referred either to the firm or a firm member by a person who has thus become acquainted with either the firm or that firm member.

Each of the following categories of firm members shall be entitled to an aliquot part of the total originating credits for fees paid by such new client: (a) the partners; (b) the firm members (including, if applicable, the partners as a group) who are, or before the application of the continuing-client rule (part E) were, entitled to the originating credits for the prior work hereinabove referred to; (c) the firm member whom the new client asks to handle his first problem (see rule B-6); and (d) any firm members who have a substantial connection with the advent of the new client that does not stem from any factor dealt with in rules B-1, B-2, or B-3. If the prior work referred to in the first sentence of this rule B-1 was performed for two or more clients, and there were two or more individual originators of them, none of whom was clearly dominant, category (b) above shall be comprised of the partners (and for this purpose, two or more related clients—see part C—are deemed to be a single client). However, if in such case one of such individual originators was clearly dominant, then category (b) shall be comprised of him or her alone. (Regarding employments and referrals by First County Bank trust officers, see rule B-9.)

Rule B-2. *Referral-Oriented New Clients.* "Referral," as used in this caption, does not relate to the referral by someone else of a client to the firm. It relates, rather, to a firm member's referring a client to a third person, to become that third person's customer or patient or client. Further, it relates only to a situation in which such referral by a firm member was made in connection with the rendition of the firm's professional service to that client. A referral-oriented new client is (1) one who has sold goods or services to one or more prior clients referred to him or her for such purchase by a firm member, or (2) one referred to the firm by such a seller of goods or services, *but only when* there appears to be a substantial inducing relationship between the aforesaid referral by a firm member and the advent of the new client. Each of the following categories of firm members shall be entitled to an aliquot part of the total originating credits for fees paid by such new client; (a) the partners, and b) any firm members who have a substantial connection with the advent of the new client that does not stem from any factor dealt with in rule B-1, B-2, or B-3. When there is no one in category (b), the entire originating credits shall be allotted to the partners.

Rule B-3. *Supplier-Oriented New Clients.* A supplier-oriented new client is (1) one who has sold goods or services to the firm, or (2) one referred to the firm by such a seller. The total originating credits for fees paid by any such new client shall be allocated as prescribed in rule B-2.

Rule B-4. *Interaction of Rules B-1 and B-2 and of B-1 and B-3.* If factors exist that call for the application of rule B-1 and also either rule B-2 or rule B-3:

(1) Rule B-1 alone shall control if the B-1 factor is the dominant one.
(2) Rule B-2 or rule B-3 alone shall control if the B-2 or B-3 factor is the dominant one.
(3) If neither of the aforesaid factors is dominant, rule B-1 shall control, but category 9b) of that rule shall be deemed to be comprised of the partners.

Rule B-5. *Overriding Influence of Independent Factor.* If a factor calling for the application of rule B-1, B-2, or B-3 exists, but at least one firm member has such a strong independent connection with the advent of a new client as to make it probable that he or she would have patronized the firm even if such factor did not exist, rule B-1, B-2, or B-3, as the case may be, shall not be applied. Originating credits for fees paid by such new client shall be allotted pursuant to the provisions of part A.

Rule B-6. *Fortuitous Events.* If a new client consults the firm and fortuitously ends up in the hands of a particular firm member, the partners shall be entitled to the aliquot part of the originating credits for fees paid by such new client that is allotted under rule B-1 to the firm member whom a new client asks to handle his first problem. If a new client initially seeks one firm member and fortuitously ends up in the hands of another firm member, the firm member initially sought, and not the other firm member, shall be entitled to the aliquot part of the originating credits for fees paid by such new client that is allotted under rule B-1 to the firm member whom a new client asked to handle his or her first problem.

Rule B-7. *Division of Aliquot Parts of Originating Credits Among Firm Members.* Any aliquot part of originating credits that is allotted to the partners in this part B shall be divided among individual partners as is provided in the firm's Income Division Plan. Any aliquot part of originating credits that is allotted to two or more firm members comprising category (b) of rule B-1 shall be divided among those firm members in the same manner as are the originating credits for fees paid by the client for whom the prior work was performed that led to the advent of the new client. Any aliquot part of originating credits that is allotted to two or more firm members comprising category (d) of rule B-1 or category (b) of rule B-2 or rule B-3 shall be divided among those firm members equally.

Rule B-8. *Employments and Referrals by First County Bank Trust Officers.* Every new client who is a trust officer of a First County bank, or who is referred by such a trust officer, is conclusively deemed to be "work-oriented." The originating credits for fees paid by such client shall be allotted one-third to the firm member, if any, whom the new client asks to handle his or her first problem, and the remaining two-thirds or three-thirds (if no individual firm members) to the partners. This rule B-8 constitutes, principally, an application of rule B-1, but it overrides every provision of these rules which is inconsistent herewith, except rule B-5 and B-6 and part E.

Part C. *Rules Applicable to Related Clients.* Notwithstanding the provisions of parts A and B, above, originating credits for fees paid by a "related client" shall be divided among individual firm members in the same manner as are the originating credits for the client to whom such "related client" is related, unless it is clearly apparent that some factor other than the relationship between the prior client and the new client was the dominant factor in the latter's advent.

Rule C-1. *Definition of Related Client.* A client is related to another client when the one is: (a) the personal representative of the other; (b) the trustee of a trust of which the other is trustor; (c) the husband, wife, parent, child, sibling, or wife of a sibling of the other or the personal representative of any such relative of the other; (d) a member of the household of the other; (e) a business entity, the selection of whose counsel is, as a practical matter and in the given instance, controlled by the other; (f) a person who, as a practical matter and in the given instance, controls the selection of the other's counsel, provided the other is a business entity; or (g) a business entity under direct or indirect common domination with another.

Part D. *De Minimus Rule.* If the aggregate of the portions of the originating credits for fees paid by any client that originally were allottable or later become allottable to any individual firm member under the provisions of parts A, B, and C of these rules is less than one-eighth of the total of such originating credits, such portion shall not be allotted to such individual firm member, but, instead, shall be allotted to the partners.

Part E. *Large Client.* Twenty-five percent (25%) of the originating credits attributable to aggregate fees collected from each client (or group of related clients) in excess of $10,000, and an additional twenty-five percent (25%) of the originating credits attributable to aggregate fees collected from each client (or group of related clients) in excess of $50,000, shall be allocated to the partners' fund, and the origination credits of the initial originator or originators reduced proportionately.

Part F. *Criminal Case Assignments.* A client whose representation by the firm or a firm member in a criminal matter arose by reason of assignment by a judge or other public official having such authority, shall be deemed to have been originated by the firm.

Part G. *Law Directory Referrals.* If the event of representation of a client by the firm or a firm member was by reason of the referral from a law list or directory (such as *Martindale-Hubbell*), the client shall be deemed to have been originated by the firm.

APPENDIX 2
Capitalization, Debt, and Taxes

Law Firm Capitalization*

by James D. Cotterman

Who will own law firms in the 21st century? Twentieth-century law firms are owned by the lawyers who work there, either as sole proprietors, partners, or shareholders. Or are they?

The legal profession in the decades following World War II generally did not rely on borrowed capital or debt. Banks did not usually lend to lawyers. The partners and proprietors provided the capital necessary to acquire the physical assets necessary to establish, run, and expand their practices. Less capital was needed for equipment. There were no computers. Operating equipment, like dictating machines and electric typewriters, and telephone systems, were simple and relatively less expensive than today. Only library expenses were at the same level. The salaries of starting lawyers were often less than those paid experienced legal secretaries, and the earnings relationship between associates and partners was much different than today, with partners earning relatively more than now.

Billing practices were less organized. Some law firms did record hours, and used them as a basis for billing clients. But many other firms billed irregularly and without a real billing philosophy. They billed in whatever way the billing lawyer viewed the value of the work performed. Many bills tended to be sent at or near year-end. A few law firms paid partners only once a year.

The 1960s and 1970s represented a transitional period, bringing about tremendous change in the economics of conducting the law business. Lawyers began to bill more often by the hour. Manual systems to record, bill, and collect for services began to become more common. Lawyers wanted to be paid for what they did. Word processing equipment was beginning to enter the legal marketplace, as were copiers and somewhat more complicated telephone systems. Lawyers were being paid more frequently and younger lawyers were beginning to have higher income expectations. Still, debt was a relatively unknown item for law firms.

**Adapted from article originally published in The Report to Legal Management, June 1990, Altman Weil Pensa Publications, Inc.*

The late 1970s and 1980s changed that. Inflation, coupled with the need to automate the office and the costs of rapid growth, enticed many law firms to use debt rather than current cash flow to acquire the necessary hard assets of practice. Inflation soared during the twenty years with four years of double-digit inflation and seven years of inflation between 5 and 10 percent. Technological change entered every facet of the legal profession. Applications proliferated into spreadsheets, databases, case management, research, calendaring, publishing, and graphics. Communications erupted with facsimile transmission, voice mail, electronic mail, and cellular telephones. Personal computers brought these applications to (or near) the desktops of each lawyer, paralegal, and secretary.

Law firms grew rapidly. In 1970, there were 355,000 lawyers; by the end of 1989 there were 725,000 lawyers. Law firms grew internally, merged and consolidated to create a few law firms of over 1,000 lawyers. Each new lawyer, on average, required a $45,000 new investment (the portion of compensation and overhead not covered by fee receipts) in the first full year and three years to recover it. Starting salaries skyrocketed as the top firms bid for the best and brightest law school graduates, up to $83,000 in New York City in 1989. Over the years the starting salary inflation spread across the country. Together, the growth in lawyers and starting salaries forced many partners to work to support the associates until the associates' cash flow would turn around two, three, or more years after hiring. As a final blow, many of the younger partners wanted the fine lifestyle that partnership was thought to mean, and therefore demanded (and got) large distributions. The more-senior partners consequently saw the relationship between their compensation and that of younger partners and associates decrease as income compression took hold.

Law firms needed capital. State laws and ethical restrictions prevented lawyers from tapping external equity sources. The solution: borrow! It became fashionable to borrow not only for physical assets, but also for growth and compensation. Leasing of everything from autos to word processors brought immediate access to equipment with little or no initial cash outlay. Accountants pushed accrual-based financial statements into the legal profession. The partners realized the vast amounts of equity tied up in the *pipeline* (unbilled time, accounts receivable) and in client costs advanced. Surely one could safely borrow against those assets to help fund the growth, to invest in space and equipment, to pay high starting salaries, and to maintain high partner compensation.

Unfortunately, for many lawyers and bankers, a large part of those assets may never be collected. The problem: unbilled time, accounts receivable, and client costs advanced can be illusory. They have no scrap or resale value. They cannot be repossessed. The fallout went public with the demise of Finley Kumble. Among its problems, the use of debt to finance partner compensation.

Partners thought they had found the answer to their capital needs and income expectations in borrowing; however, that solution, as implemented in many firms, may backfire. How should law firms manage their balance sheets and capital needs? The basic financial management tool is the budget. Many law firms do not do an adequate job of budgeting the income statement; most do not even try to budget a balance sheet. With a mixture of accounting methods for financial statements and generally unsophisticated financial acumen in the legal profession, it is often difficult to do much more than rely on general rules of thumb. What guidelines are available and how reliable are they?

The first place to look for guidelines are the people who lend money for a living—the bankers. The market for law firm banking services has grown to the point that major banks have designated specialized groups that focus on law firms. Even though the banking profession is partly to blame for the debt problem, it can also be a source of information. Bankers look to the ability to be repaid as the prime factor in the extension of credit. To determine this ability, bankers generally look to several statistics:

Total debt less than 80 percent* of total distributable income;
Total debt less than 80 percent* of current collectible (usually defined as less than 120 days old) accounts receivable and unbilled time;
30-day cleanup of lines of credit;
Occupancy costs less than 10 percent of gross fees received;
Stable ownership group; and
Profiles of gross receipts per lawyer, average partner income, and per partner equity.

As consultants to the legal profession, we advise against any borrowing that extends much beyond the acquisition of fixed assets. In effect, you should maintain positive equity (capital) on the cash basis. The first law of management is, *do not borrow money to pay the partners or shareholders*. The only exception to this law is to zero out profits at year-end in a professional corporation/association. Even then, the debt should be repaid in full by the end of the first quarter of the following year. Working capital debt should be zero for at least ninety days during the year and at year-end. This could be achieved by cleaning up the credit line for one week each month.

Some law firms now have a painful path to fiscal health. Borrowing may need to be curtailed. Partner incomes may be adversely affected while the law firm repays prior excesses. Unfunded obligations to withdrawing partners may need to be revisited. All this at a time when the legal profession is losing its ability to grow out of trouble. As the legal profession looks toward the next century, the signs of a maturing marketplace point toward increased competition. That, in turn, leads to reduced profitability. Firms with heavy debt burdens may be hard pressed to maintain or improve their competitive advantage. Those law firms who borrow to pay themselves may find a banker on their doorstep holding the keys.

Debt and Taxes

The preceding discussion on capitalization and borrowing to pay partner compensation raised financial issues; many law firms face potential tax difficulties in this process as well.

Partnerships

A partner computes taxable income on his or her share of partnership income and the pass-through items of deduction and credit. The partner receives a K-1 from the law firm summarizing this information. The partner does not receive a W-2, as employees do, because a partner is not an employee, but rather is self-employed. The cash distributions a partner

*The author, however, would not recommend borrowing up to this standard.

receives from the law firm partnership may or may not correlate with the taxable income he or she must report to the Internal Revenue Service.

For example, if a partnership borrows $500,000 and distributes the funds to the partners, the transaction has no income tax effect for the partnership or the partners. *The partners are jointly and severally liable for repayment of the partnership debt*. Interest paid for use of the fund is a partnership expense, and hence deductible.

The good news: The partners receive the money free from income taxes. The bad news: When the partnership repays the bank, it uses fee receipts, which normally are used for current operations and partner draws. This reduces the monies available for partner distributions. The repayment of the loan is not a partnership expense. The partners report taxable income on the funds that were paid to the bank. For some partners, the prior year windfall has already been spent, and the tax bill represents a financial hardship. As stated above, all of the partners are liable for repayments of the debt.

Corporations

If a professional corporation borrows $500,000 and distributes the funds to the shareholders, the payments to the shareholders represent compensation that is deductible by the professional corporation and *taxable income* to the shareholders. The shareholders pay income taxes on the funds, most likely at 31 percent or 39.6 percent for federal, plus any state and local income taxes. The professional corporation pays interest on the full amount borrowed. Interest is deductible.

This technique is used by many professional corporations to eliminate taxable income at year-end. Such actions are necessary because of differing loan amortization and fixed asset depreciation schedules or miscalculations in planning. When used, the funds should be repaid in the first quarter of the following year to minimize interest costs. Until the depreciation/amortization imbalance or other problems reverse, this use of debt will be necessary.

If, however, the borrowed funds were simply an advance against future income, there will come the day of reckoning when the borrowed funds must be repaid, creating taxable income at the corporate level. The worst possible situation would be that the professional corporation would have to pay the current 35 percent corporate federal income tax, plus any state and local levies. The shareholders would not only have reduced current income from the debt repayment, but also the knowledge that the taxing authorities have between one-third and one-half of the original principal in addition. Such use of debt only results in a shifting of taxable income from one year to another, and increases the tax burden drastically, since the borrowed funds were taxed at individual rates, and the repaid amounts may be taxed at the personal service corporation rate of 35 percent.

APPENDIX 3
Retirement Planning Primer

Law firms, like all organizations, must deal with the issue of whether current cash should be set aside to provide for the accumulation of retirement assets for their workers. No matter the size of the organization, the potential dollars are enormous. And given the current and projected severe government resource constraints, the need to accumulate assets for the post-employment years becomes even more important.

For law firm owners, the establishment of funded retirement programs represents a direct reduction to the current compensation of the owners. Only plans that provide for individual employee contributions spread this financial impact further. The following primer is to provide an overview of retirement and discuss the impact of unfunded plans on the profession. The authors hope that it encourages further reading on the topic and stimulates an educational process for all employees within the organization.

This primer is adapted from several articles produced by the authors over the past several years, as well as from data compiled in its surveys of the profession regarding this topic. It should serve as an introduction to the topic and begin the process necessary to bring one's own plans into line with expectations and economic reality.

"Can I personally afford to retire?" "Can we afford to pay the retirement?" These questions are commonly asked by senior and younger partners, respectively, as they begin to grapple with issues of retirement and buy-out. Survey information is provided on unfunded obligations, qualified retirement plans, retirement ages, valuation and return of capital, vesting requirements, eligibility requirements, and payout terms. Comparisons to data collected from studies conducted in 1981, 1984, 1989, and 1993 are also presented.

Responses to survey questions varied most by firm size. Differences by form of organization were most often a result of the influence size has on a law firm's form of organization. Professional corporations are far more prevalent among small law firms.

Formal Retirement Policies

Not every law firm has formal documentation (partnership agreement or corporate bylaws, shareholders' agreement, and employment contracts). Not every agreement speaks to the issue of retirement. Formal documentation and the existence of a retirement clause continue to increase in prevalence with firm size. Only one firm in five with fewer than twenty lawyers had a formal retirement policy. Conversely, four firms out of five with one hundred or more lawyers had formalized their retirement policies. Overall, only 55 percent of firms have documented retirement provisions, down from 62 percent in 1989.

Retirement Age

Mandatory retirement is one of the more emotional withdrawal issues. Since 1981, there have been two significant changes in the laws affecting retirement age. The first is the 1986 amendment to the Age Discrimination in Employment Act of 1967 (ADEA), as amended through 1978, which generally prohibits mandatory retirement provisions applied to an employee over age forty. The employer must have twenty or more employees. Partners are not covered by the Act, but Shareholder employees of PCs are. The second is the Social Security amendments of 1983, which increased the age under which full retirement benefits would be available from ages sixty-five to sixty-seven and reduced early retirement benefits.

The incidence of a mandatory retirement age has risen to 40 percent of the firms surveyed, compared to 34 percent in 1989. As in the past studies, the incidence increases with firm size. For those firms with a mandatory retirement age, age seventy reigns supreme, as it has in all three prior studies.

Return of Capital

The return of capital in law firms (repurchase of stock in professional corporations) is, for most firms, a minor amount. Only 10 percent of the firms surveyed indicated that they use the accrual method of valuing capital. Seventy-four percent of the law firms use the cash income tax basis. The rest use fixed capital values, modified cash basis valuation, or a combination of valuation methods.

Qualified Retirement Plans

IRS qualified retirement plans have decreased slightly in popularity since the 1989 study (93 percent) to 88 percent of the firms reporting such plans. However, they increased dramatically over the 1984 study, where only 69 percent of the firms had adopted such plans. Small law firms (under twenty lawyers) remain as the least likely to adopt such plans with only 70 percent of such firms reporting qualified retirement plans.

In 1982, TEFRA (Tax Equity and Fiscal Responsibility Act) eliminated all substantive differences between the retirement plans available for the self-employed and corporate employees. This opened up massive benefits to proprietorships, partnerships, and S corporations.

Such *funded* retirement programs, where the availability of retirement assets is assured by setting aside current income as it is earned and before the payment of personal income taxes, had been an absolute winner for many law firms. High tax rates and more liberal deferral and exclusion rules made it possible for law firm owners to save more in taxes than contributions for nonowners cost. Because of changes in the tax laws in 1986, however, nearly one-quarter of the respondents had or were planning to discontinue them. After 1986, the tax laws and rate structure eliminated the absolute dollar savings partners previously were able to achieve with qualified plans. It costs the partners money to include associates and support staff.

Unfunded Obligations

Unfunded obligations represent a fundamental risk to the legal profession in an era of partner mobility, low or no growth in timekeepers, an aging lawyer population, and severe pricing constraints from clients in a very competitive market. The history of unfunded obligations goes back to an era before professional corporations, before qualified retirement plans, before ERISA, and in some cases, before Social Security old-age benefits. It was an era of relatively easy profits, and rapid growth in both lawyers and legal business. Ownership structures were stable. The proportion of the profession benefiting from these obligations were few when compared to the number providing the profits from which the benefits were paid.

Unfunded entitlements, which rely on the ability and willingness of future owners to pay the benefits set forth in such plans, continue with some popularity. Because the assumptions of ability and willingness are currently under question in many law firms, however (thanks in large part to the changing demographics of the legal profession), substantially fewer law firms have unfunded plans today than in 1981.

Example: Social Security

A large scale example of the legal profession's problem is seen in the Social Security system. Social Security was established in 1935 on a pay-as-you-go funding approach. Current workers contribute to the funds as they earn. Benefits for retired, deceased, and disabled workers are paid out of those funds. Active workers' contributions are individually low because of the relationship between the large number of contributors and the smaller number of beneficiaries. Table A-1 shows the relationship of the contributors (working population, age eighteen to sixty-four) and the beneficiaries (sixty-five and older) from 1940 to the year 2010. As demonstrated in the table, the relationship between contributors and beneficiaries is changing dramatically.

Two other phenomena affect the viability of a pay-as-you-go approach. First is the traditional retirement age of sixty-five. The ADEA, discussed earlier, prohibited age-based mandatory retirement, but the expected lengthening of work life did not occur. In fact, average retirement age decreased. In 1963, 46 percent of the age-sixty-five male labor force was retired. In 1985, the proportion of retirees had increased to 70 percent.* The contributors are electing to retire early and collect benefits longer.

TABLE A-1 **Population Demographics**

	1940	*1990*	*2010*
Contributors	58.7%	61.7%	63.8%
Beneficiaries	6.9%	12.6%	14.0%
Percent of total population	65.6%	74.3%	77.8%
Ratio of contributors to beneficiaries	8.5:1	4.9:1	4.6:1

*Source: Adapted from Packard & Reno (1988).

The second phenomenon is the lengthening life span of Americans. Beneficiaries are living longer. Life expectancy for a sixty-five-year-old male in 1940 was approximately twelve additional years. By 1985, male life expectancy at age sixty-five had increased to fifteen years. By the year 2010, this is projected to increase to twenty years. In all cases, females are expected to live longer and the life span differences are increasing. The combination of early retirement and lengthened lives substantially increases the benefits that are ultimately required to be paid.

During the 1980s, the federal government realized that workers would probably be unwilling and unable to afford contributions for the projected benefit stream in the twenty-first century. A solution was designed that combined changes in the calculation of benefit increases, changes in the age of availability of benefits, and changes in the method of funding for benefits. The funding change provided for increased contributions now to provide reserves to pay for benefits in the twenty-first century.

The Legal Profession

The legal profession faces the same demographic issues.[†] The profession is aging and more women are rising through the ranks. In 1988, 16 percent of the lawyers in the United States were women; while in 1992, 43 percent of the law school graduating class were female. This is particularly important given the statistics on life span for women.

Moreover, law firms are experiencing burgeoning independence in the lawyer ranks. Lawyers (associates and partners) are "jumping ship" with increasing frequency. The legal market is extremely competitive and Model Rule for Professional Conduct 5.6 (formerly DR2-108) effectively allows partners and shareholders in law firms to change firms and take their clients with them whenever they choose to do so. As a result, partners or shareholders with a book of business that would entitle them to greater compensation elsewhere frequently leave their firms. The result is that most frequently the most productive partners or shareholders defect, along with their revenue streams, placing a firm in severe jeopardy. What's left behind in many cases are the liabilities for debt and office space that now must be shared by a smaller group. This is not an environment in which one should entrust one's successors with one's financial retirement entitlements.

Indeed, it is still not uncommon for Altman Weil Pensa, Inc., to be called in to assist a firm that has no retirement provisions for its partners. These law firms often have senior members who expected to "die with their boots on," earning sufficient levels of income to maintain their lifestyle and status. The partners frequently have inadequate personal resources to retire; the firm has no qualified vehicle funded for such purpose; and the younger members are faced with what can be overwhelming financial obligations. The issue for many firms is that while they comprehend the problem, they are unable to chart a more appropriate approach to provide for this income later in life.

It is helpful here to review the available sources of retirement income. A retired partner can generate income from four sources: 1) Social Security

---

[†]See Weil, R., *The Aging of the Profession; Report to Legal Management*, Altman Weil Pensa Publications, Inc., Newtown Square, PA, May 1990.

benefits, 2) employer (law firm) retirement plans, 3) personal savings and investments, and 4) post-retirement employment. In all but the mega-law firms, sources two and three are essentially the same. If employer-mandated plans are established, however, there is a far greater likelihood that a retiring partner will have financial assets for retirement. Lawyers, like most Americans, often find substantial personal saving a very difficult habit to cultivate.

Many law firms have structured programs for senior members of the firm to continue working in a reduced capacity. The most-often-used term describing such positions is *of counsel*. Some firms simply provide an office for a retired senior member and minimal secretarial support. There may be no requirements for the position. Individuals function as uncompensated "elder statesmen" of the firm.

At the other extreme are positions with expectations regarding hours, fees generated, or business developed. Compensation can be a salary or percentage of fees. Individually negotiated contracts are common. Care must be taken in combining compensated of counsel arrangements with other deferred compensation entitlements. An error could subject the deferred compensation to FICA tax and interfere with the receipt of Social Security benefits.

What options are available in retirement planning? What may work for one firm, of course, could be devastating in another. For some, a combination of solutions, where different approaches are bundled to meet the needs and expectations of the partners, may be required.

Alternatives

There are two broad approaches to retirement planning: qualified and nonqualified plans. A basic understanding of the differences between the two is important. Qualified plans are highly regulated under Internal Revenue and Labor Department rules. These plans provide for preferential tax treatment of contributions (immediate deduction) and benefits (tax deferred and special treatment at distribution) in exchange for broad coverage and nondiscrimination provisions. Plan earnings accumulate tax free and plan assets must be secured (placed outside the reach of the employer and creditors). The drawbacks of qualified plans are reporting, disclosure, and other regulatory considerations. They are typically expensive to administer, particularly defined benefit plans that require the services of an actuary and payment of pension benefit insurance premiums. There is also the cost of covering nonlawyer employees of the firm. The current coverage and nondiscrimination rules protect nonhighly compensated employees and prohibit the one employee professional corporation plans formerly available.

Who is considered a highly compensated employee? As usual, it depends. The following three limitations are used in the highly compensated employee definition (limits are for 1995 and are adjusted for inflation):

- Any employee with pay greater than $100,000,
- Employees in the top-paid group (top 20 percent) earning more than $66,000, or
- Officers with pay equal to or greater than $60,000.

Nonqualified plans, as their name implies, do not qualify for preferential tax treatment under the tax laws (no immediate deduction or deferral). Earnings can accumulate tax-free only if a life insurance product is used. On the other hand, they are unhindered by the coverage and nondiscrimination regulations that affect qualified plans. One may discriminate, selecting for whom and how much the firm is willing to accrue benefits. Such programs do not carry the reporting and disclosure burdens of qualified plans (a simple one-time disclosure filing is required with the Department of Labor). They also lack the security of assets that a qualified plan may provide.

Advantage of Tax Sheltering

An example of the financial implications of these qualified versus nonqualified savings plans is shown in Table A-2. It examines the result of saving $30,000 per year for ten years under both a qualified and a nonqualified plan (personal savings). A funded nonqualified plan would not be practical in a law firm (particularly professional corporations). Professional corporations would be disadvantaged because of the corporate tax on retained income and its effect on shareholder-employee current compensation. The partnership would have economies similar to personal savings.

It is clear that the qualified plan provides for a significantly higher accumulation that, upon distribution, is subject to tax. Favorable federal income tax rules, however, lower the effective tax rate that would otherwise be applied, and some states do not levy income taxes on retirement benefits.

Many law firms are now finding, however, that the changes in income tax rates have changed the economics of qualified plans. A secondary benefit to deferring taxation of compensation and earnings had historically been that the retiree would most likely be in a lower marginal income tax bracket upon retirement than when the income was earned. The current income tax rate structure makes this less likely. There is also a reasonable expectation that marginal income tax rates will continue to rise, as will also the number of tax brackets. The income tax rate structure at the time of income deferral, the length of time income is deferred, and the expected income tax rate structure at distribution affect retirement contribution planning. Current low income tax rate structures have also increased the cost of covering nonowners, relative to the tax benefit received by partners. Still, many plans can be integrated with Social Security, reducing the costs of covering lower-paid employees.

TABLE A-2 **Qualified vs. Nonqualified Plans**

Savings Description	*Qualified Plan*	*Nonqualified Plan*
Sum available	$ 30,000	$ 30,000
Income taxes at 37%*	0	11,100
Net amount invested	$ 30,000	$ 18,900
Earnings of 8% on investment	$ 2,400	$ 1,512
Income taxes at 37% on earnings	0	560
Net accumulated first year	$ 32,400	$ 19,852
At end of ten years	$469,365	$250,170

*Federal income tax rate of 31%, plus estimated state/local income taxes of 6%.

Nonqualified Plans

The traditional retirement "plan" in many law firms consists of a return of capital and an interest in unbilled time and accounts receivable. Today, most firms with such plans have turned to a percentage of past earnings as the primary valuation of entitlement, in addition to a return of capital. Other primary valuation methods include a percentage/point interest in firm income or a flat dollar amount. Regardless of valuation method, when compared to current partner earnings, the value of the benefit is typically a multiple of one-half to one-and-one-half times the individual's earnings. Funding of such plans is rare. However, cost containment caps and service requirements are not. Benefits payments cover the gamut from lump sum to life annuity for the beneficiary and spouse.

Many law firm plans that provide for cost containment caps look to limit total benefits paid in any one year. Such limits protect the firm from swings in profitability and the burden of expanding numbers of beneficiaries. Rarely do they limit overall costs.

These plans are often represented by *unsecured* promises. In essence, the retiree relies on the moral commitment, survival, and financial ability of the firm to honor these agreements.

Many law firms are realizing that unfunded plans are financial time bombs set to explode early in the next century. This is when the current group of thirty-five to fifty-year-old lawyers will be ready for retirement.

Qualified Plan Options

Qualified plans represent the best approach available under existing tax law. The recent tax law changes have, again, made accumulation of retirement assets more difficult and expensive. For 1993, compensation of up to $235,840 could be considered for purposes of determining contributions and benefits. This number, originally $200,000 in 1988, was indexed for inflation annually. In 1994, new legislation lowered that limit to $150,000 and beginning in 1995, it will be indexed for inflation only in $10,000 increments. Table A-3* provides some indication of the potential impact of this change in the law.

TABLE A-3 **Impact of Tax Law Changes on Qualified Plans**[1]

	Years to Retirement	
Annual Contribution	*25 Years*	*15 Years*
$30,000	$2,368,632	$879,728
$22,500	1,776,474	659,796
Reduction in account balance	$ 592,158	$219,932

[1]This example assumes an 8 percent annual return and no increase in the compensation limit or annual addition limits.

*Adapted from Research Institute of America (1993).

In addition, by lowering eligible compensation, the percentage deferred by very highly compensated individuals increases. This widens the spread of average deferrals between nonhighly and highly compensated individuals. The result may be to require additional reduction in deferrals by highly compensated individuals.

What may scare off some people is the maze of names: defined benefit, defined contribution, profit sharing, target benefit, 401(k), money purchase, Keogh, and pension. A short review should place everyone in a position to intelligently review these options.

There are essentially two forms of organization that law firms utilize: incorporated (professional corporation/association) and unincorporated (sole proprietorship, partnership). Qualified plans available to corporate forms of organization are *corporate plans*. Qualified plans for unincorporated businesses are *Keogh plans*. All plans offer nearly the same features. There are minor differences in that Keogh plans are not permitted to have loan provisions for more than 10-percent owners, and contributions are based on self-employed earnings. Corporate plans permit limited plan loan provisions and contributions are based on salary and bonus.

The following outline puts order to the maze of titles in qualified plans.

KEOGH	***CORPORATE***
Defined benefit	Defined benefit
Target benefit	Target benefit
Money purchase	Money purchase
Profit sharing	Profit sharing
401(k)	401(k)
SEP	SEP

Many of the titles in qualified retirement plans are used indiscriminately. The following illustrates the proper family groupings of the various qualified plans available to law firms.

DEFINED BENEFIT

Defined benefit

DEFINED CONTRIBUTION

Target benefit
Money purchase
Profit sharing
401(k)
SEP

PENSION

Defined benefit
Target benefit
Money purchase

PROFIT SHARING

Profit sharing
Age-weighted profit sharing
401(k)

Defined Benefit Plans

Defined benefit plans specify the benefit that the retiree will receive based on age, years of service, and past earnings. The plan assets are insured by the Pension Benefit Guaranty Corporation (a federal agency under ERISA), and assets of the trust are lumped together with no individual accounting. Forfeitures remain in the trust to reduce future costs. The benefit can be calculated under several different formulae; unit benefit and flat percentage of earnings (often final average) are two common formulae. These plans benefit older individuals in that they recognize past service and fund for a determined benefit.

Actuaries are needed to establish the funding required to provide adequate reserves from which to pay the retiree. Maximum benefits are currently $120,000 (1995) per year and are indexed to inflation. The risk of investment performance and inflation lie with the employer (law firm). Accordingly, the costs of funding the plans are not readily determinable without the help of an actuary. You can ensure a significant benefit quickly for older individuals, but often at high cost. Contributions to the plan are skewed disproportionately towards older individuals with longer service histories. Such plans can be used effectively to replace unfunded obligations if their cost is counted as general overhead rather than attributed to the participants.

Defined Contribution Plans

Defined contribution plans focus on individual accounting for contributions. Benefit amounts are not guaranteed nor insured. The risk of investment performance and inflation lie with the administrator and the individual. Maximum contributions are the lesser of 25 percent of salary or $30,000. These contribution limits are also indexed to inflation. Because contributions are based on compensation, potential benefits are based on career average earnings. Costs are predictable. These plans work well for younger individuals who have a lot of time to accumulate retirement funds.

Four types of plans warrant special discussion: target benefit, profit sharing, 401(k), and SEP (simplified employee pension). Target benefit plans are hybrids of the defined benefit and defined contribution plans. The plan is a defined contribution plan where the contributions are actuarially determined to provide a *target* benefit. The benefit is not guaranteed; exposure for investment performance and inflation rests with the employee. Essentially, it allows for greater funding of benefits for older employees and longer serviced employees (owners), while costing less than a true defined benefit plan.

Profit-sharing plans are flexible in that annual contributions by the employer are not required and amounts can vary. Total contributions are limited by law to 15 percent of payroll and a *profit* is not required by law for contributions to be made. Profitability, however, can be required by the employer in structuring contribution requirements for the plans. Employee withdrawals are possible two years after contribution by the employer if the plan is so written. A formula determining the allocation of funds to participants must be set forth. Allocation formulas can reflect compensation and length of service and age (age-weighted profit-sharing plans came about in early 1992 when final regulations under IRC Section 401(a)(4) were issued).

401(k) plans are very popular. They allow a participant to defer current taxation on a portion of his or her compensation (the 1995 maximum is $9,240). These plans can be established as profit sharing, salary reduction, or thrift plans. Special nondiscrimination rules apply to prevent abuse by highly compensated individuals; however, these plans require a minimum number of voluntary participants from among the support staff. They are administratively complex.

SEP (simplified employee pension) is another specialized defined contribution plan. Contributions are made to an individual retirement account for each employee. Maximum contributions are the lesser of 15 percent of compensation or $30,000. SEPs are administratively simple with little cost to maintain. Because contributions go to individual retirement accounts, the law firm avoids investment and distribution control and liability. As such, termination requires no paperwork and no annual reports are required. 401(k) and integration with Social Security are permitted features under certain circumstances. Although contributions are discretionary, participation and vesting requirements are strict (part-timers must be included).

What to Do

What should law firms do to deal with this whole area? Retirement planning for law firms should begin with a review of existing arrangements, including all related issues of buy-in, buy-out, capitalization, and compensation. Treatment of the funding for retirement and its interrelationship with current compensation entitlement is critical.

There are two general approaches. Such contributions can be considered as part of general overhead (before the profit pie is split). Alternatively, contributions can be included in an individual partner's total compensation. Partners should be surveyed as to their understanding and preferences. Questionnaires and confidential interviews are appropriate ways to solicit partner input into the process. An actuary will be needed to provide the costs for defined benefit and target benefit plans. It is best to employ an independent consultant experienced in law firms and retirement planning to develop an appropriate structure.

It is common to hear law firm partners say that they are satisfied with the status quo—they then defer action. But the cost of waiting to begin planning for retirement is high. The ability to accumulate substantial assets and overcome inflation or less than spectacular investment performance is greatest when the individual is under age forty. Many lawyers do not seriously consider the importance of retirement planning, however, until they are in their late forties or fifties.

The following example depicts the cost of delay in dealing with retirement planning. Assume that a partner wants to provide for an annual retirement income of $75,000 (in today's dollars) at age sixty-five. The partner estimates that Social Security benefits will provide a portion of the total annual income. Estimates used in this projection are based on age, earnings, and Social Security Administration data. (Individual estimates are available by contacting the Social Security Administration.)

The partner expects to need income to age ninety-five. This will provide a high degree of confidence that income will be available during the retiree and spouse's lifetime. The partner estimates that pre- and post-retirement inflation will average 3.5 percent annually. (This is approximately the average inflation rate over the past sixty years.) In order to maintain constant buying power, the retirement income required at age sixty-five is adjusted for inflation, and the annual retirement benefit is increased 3.5 percent per year. It is not important to this partner to provide a sizable estate; therefore, the principal will be liquidated by age ninety-five. The partner expects to earn a real (inflation adjusted) after-tax return of 4.0 percent on pre-retirement assets. A more conservative 2.0 percent real after-tax return is expected post-retirement.

Description	***Age 35***	***Age 45***	***Age 55***
Single lump sum today to provide benefits	$406,000	$614,000	$927,000
Annual level contributions required	32,000	56,000	126,000
Amount of first contribution if graduated with contributions rising at 3.5% annually	22,000	43,000	109,000

As can be seen, providing for retirement is a serious issue that should be dealt with early. Delay only serves to make choices more limited and much more costly. Law firms with unfunded plans should review them with the goal of providing a more financially sound package without sacrificing vested interests of senior members of the firm.

APPENDIX 4

Who Are Exempt Employees?

There are four categories of employees who are exempt under the Fair Labor Standards Act of 1936: (1) executive, (2) administrative, (3) professional, and (4) outside sales. The basic criteria for defining exempt employees are (1) duties and responsibilities and (2) amount of salary. A title or payment of salary does not determine exempt status. To be classified as exempt, an employee must meet *all* of the criteria in a category, as shown on the following page.

	Executive	Administrative	Professional	Outside Sales
Primary duties	Management of the enterprise or recognized subdivision.	Nonmanual work directly related to general policies and operations or responsible work related to education or training.	Advanced knowledge requiring instruction, or original and creative work in a recognized artistic field, or certified teacher or recognized instructor.	Customarily and regularly work away from place of business selling or obtaining orders for goods or services.
Other duties	Customarily and regularly direct two or more employees. Authority to hire and fire or to recommend either with particular weight, to avoid confusion and customarily and regularly exercise discretionary powers.	Customarily and regularly exercise discretion, independent judgment, and authority for important decisions. Regularly assist a proprietor, executive, or administrator, or perform under general supervision requiring special skills or perform special assignments under general supervision.	Customarily and regularly exercise discretion and judgment. Work is predominantly intellectual and varied rather than routine or mechanical.	
Time requirement	20% of time can be spent on nonmanagerial duties, 40% for service or retail establishment.	20% of time can be spent on nonadministrative duties, 40% for service or retail establishments.	20% of time can be spent on nonprofessional duties.	20% of time can be spent on type of work done by nonexempt employees.
Salary requirement	At least $155/week other than board, lodging, or other facilities.	At least $155/week other than board, lodging, or other facilities.	At least $170/week other than board, lodging, or other facilities.	None.
Short test for high salary (20% test does not apply if salary is greater than)	At $250/week, 20% rule above changes to: majority of time must be spent on managerial duties.	At $250/week, 20% rule above changes to: majority of time must be spent on managerial duties.	At $250/week, 20% rule above changes to: majority of time must be spent on managerial duties.	

APPENDIX 5
Compensation Survey

OCCUPATIONAL COMPENSATION SURVEY: PAY ONLY
(Philadelphia, Pennsylvania–New Jersey Metropolitan Area, November 1992)

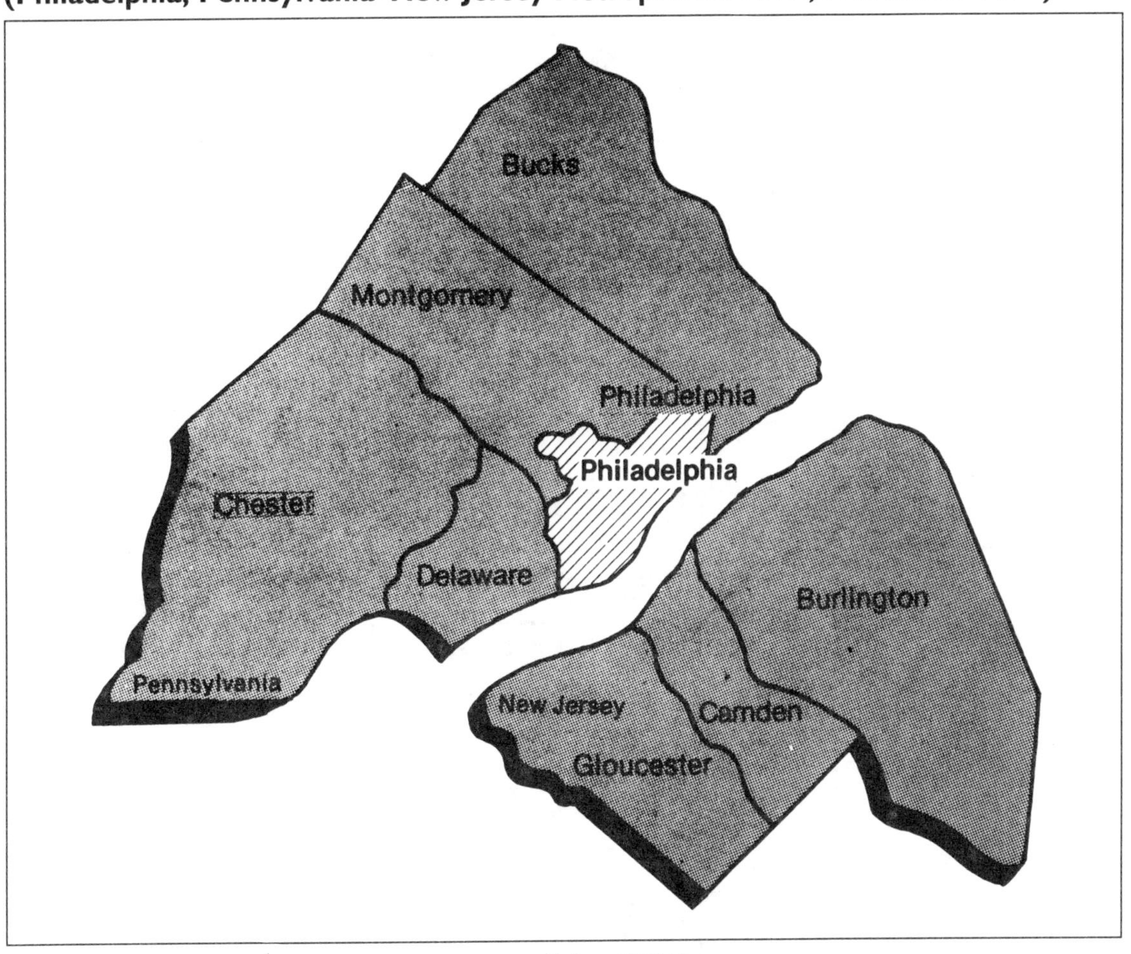

Source: U.S. Department of Labor, Bureau of Labor Statistics, Bulletin 3065-71.

Table A-1. All establishments: Weekly hours and earnings of professional and administrative occupations, Philadelphia, PA-NJ, November 1992

Occupation and level	Number of workers	Average weekly hours[1] (standard)	Weekly earnings (in dollars)[2]			Percent of workers receiving straight-time weekly earnings (in dollars) of—																					
			Mean	Median	Middle range	300 and under 400	400 - 500	500 - 600	600 - 700	700 - 800	800 - 900	900 - 1000	1000 - 1100	1100 - 1200	1200 - 1300	1300 - 1400	1400 - 1500	1500 - 1600	1600 - 1700	1700 - 1800	1800 - 1900	1900 - 2000	2000 - 2100	2100 - 2200	2200 - 2300	2300 and over
Professional Occupations																											
Accountants																											
Level I	540	38.9	$478	$480	$450 – $507	5	65	27	2	(3)	–	–	–	–	–	–	–	–	–	–	–	–	–	–	–	–
Private industry	514	38.9	478	480	450 – 509	6	64	28	2	(3)	–	–	–	–	–	–	–	–	–	–	–	–	–	–	–	–
Goods producing	112	38.7	521	515	488 – 555	5	26	57	11	1	–	–	–	–	–	–	–	–	–	–	–	–	–	–	–	–
Manufacturing	112	38.7	521	515	488 – 555	5	26	57	11	1	–	–	–	–	–	–	–	–	–	–	–	–	–	–	–	–
Service producing	402	38.9	466	467	450 – 494	6	75	19	–	–	–	–	–	–	–	–	–	–	–	–	–	–	–	–	–	–
State and local government	26	39.9	475	–	– – –	–	81	19	–	–	–	–	–	–	–	–	–	–	–	–	–	–	–	–	–	–
Level II	1,373	38.8	569	557	528 – 605	(3)	13	59	23	4	1	–	–	–	–	–	–	–	–	–	–	–	–	–	–	–
Private industry	1,281	38.8	569	557	528 – 605	(3)	13	60	22	4	1	–	–	–	–	–	–	–	–	–	–	–	–	–	–	–
Goods producing	456	39.5	581	566	530 – 618	(3)	9	50	31	8	1	–	–	–	–	–	–	–	–	–	–	–	–	–	–	–
Manufacturing	454	39.5	582	569	530 – 618	(3)	9	50	31	8	1	–	–	–	–	–	–	–	–	–	–	–	–	–	–	–
Service producing	825	38.4	562	549	526 – 599	–	15	66	16	2	(3)	–	–	–	–	–	–	–	–	–	–	–	–	–	–	–
State and local government	92	38.8	564	553	528 – 605	–	15	48	36	1	–	–	–	–	–	–	–	–	–	–	–	–	–	–	–	–
Level III	1,417	38.9	720	712	657 – 770	–	(3)	6	37	41	12	3	1	–	–	–	–	–	–	–	–	–	–	–	–	–
Private industry	1,307	39.0	719	712	657 – 770	–	–	6	36	43	13	2	1	–	–	–	–	–	–	–	–	–	–	–	–	–
Goods producing	518	39.5	742	737	678 – 787	–	–	2	25	50	20	2	–	–	–	–	–	–	–	–	–	–	–	–	–	–
Manufacturing	518	39.5	742	737	678 – 787	–	–	2	25	50	20	2	–	–	–	–	–	–	–	–	–	–	–	–	–	–
Service producing	789	38.6	704	691	643 – 749	–	–	8	43	38	7	1	2	–	–	–	–	–	–	–	–	–	–	–	–	–
Transportation and utilities	64	38.7	840	834	682 – 1,009	–	–	–	27	20	13	11	30	–	–	–	–	–	–	–	–	–	–	–	–	–
State and local government	110	38.7	722	663	663 – 779	–	1	2	57	24	–	16	–	–	–	–	–	–	–	–	–	–	–	–	–	–
Level IV	727	38.8	953	960	851 – 1,040	–	–	(3)	1	8	30	27	22	12	1	–	–	–	–	–	–	–	–	–	–	–
Private industry	661	38.9	962	960	870 – 1,046	–	–	–	1	7	27	28	23	13	1	–	–	–	–	–	–	–	–	–	–	–
Goods producing	328	39.3	986	960	894 – 1,078	–	–	–	–	5	22	30	20	20	2	–	–	–	–	–	–	–	–	–	–	–
Manufacturing	255	39.1	968	952	889 – 1,040	–	–	–	–	7	28	24	26	13	3	–	–	–	–	–	–	–	–	–	–	–
Service producing	333	38.4	938	950	845 – 1,037	–	–	–	2	8	32	27	25	7	(3)	–	–	–	–	–	–	–	–	–	–	–
Transportation and utilities	35	39.8	892	–	– – –	–	–	–	–	23	51	6	6	11	3	–	–	–	–	–	–	–	–	–	–	–
State and local government	66	38.7	862	826	826 – 881	–	–	2	–	17	58	8	17	–	–	–	–	–	–	–	–	–	–	–	–	–
Level V	128	38.5	1,216	1,233	1,133 – 1,304	–	–	–	–	–	1	6	13	24	30	15	10	–	–	–	–	–	–	–	–	–
Private industry	112	38.6	1,240	1,248	1,144 – 1,362	–	–	–	–	–	–	2	14	21	35	17	12	–	–	–	–	–	–	–	–	–
Goods producing	58	39.6	1,242	–	– – –	–	–	–	–	–	–	–	16	17	34	31	2	–	–	–	–	–	–	–	–	–
Manufacturing	58	39.6	1,242	–	– – –	–	–	–	–	–	–	–	16	17	34	31	2	–	–	–	–	–	–	–	–	–
Service producing	54	37.5	1,237	–	– – –	–	–	–	–	–	–	4	13	24	35	2	22	–	–	–	–	–	–	–	–	–
Accountants, Public																											
Level I	316	39.9	534	538	492 – 576	–	25	72	3	–	–	–	–	–	–	–	–	–	–	–	–	–	–	–	–	–
Private industry	316	39.9	534	538	492 – 576	–	25	72	3	–	–	–	–	–	–	–	–	–	–	–	–	–	–	–	–	–
Service producing	316	39.9	534	538	492 – 576	–	25	72	3	–	–	–	–	–	–	–	–	–	–	–	–	–	–	–	–	–
Level II	529	40.6	627	622	560 – 662	–	7	33	40	13	6	–	–	–	–	–	–	–	–	–	–	–	–	–	–	–
Private industry	529	40.6	627	622	560 – 662	–	7	33	40	13	6	–	–	–	–	–	–	–	–	–	–	–	–	–	–	–
Service producing	529	40.6	627	622	560 – 662	–	7	33	40	13	6	–	–	–	–	–	–	–	–	–	–	–	–	–	–	–
Level III	425	39.8	671	643	599 – 725	–	1	27	42	17	5	8	–	–	–	–	–	–	–	–	–	–	–	–	–	–
Private industry	425	39.8	671	643	599 – 725	–	1	27	42	17	5	8	–	–	–	–	–	–	–	–	–	–	–	–	–	–
Service producing	425	39.8	671	643	599 – 725	–	1	27	42	17	5	8	–	–	–	–	–	–	–	–	–	–	–	–	–	–

See footnotes at end of table.

Table A-1. All establishments: Weekly hours and earnings of professional and administrative occupations, Philadelphia, PA-NJ, November 1992 — Continued

Occupation and level	Number of workers	Average weekly hours[1] (standard)	Weekly earnings (in dollars)[2]			Percent of workers receiving straight-time weekly earnings (in dollars) of—																				
			Mean	Median	Middle range	300 and under 400	400 - 500	500 - 600	600 - 700	700 - 800	800 - 900	900 - 1000	1000 - 1100	1100 - 1200	1200 - 1300	1300 - 1400	1400 - 1500	1500 - 1600	1600 - 1700	1700 - 1800	1800 - 1900	1900 - 2000	2000 - 2100	2100 - 2200	2200 - 2300	2300 and over
Level IV	371	39.5	$1,196	$1,209	$1,081 – $1,289	–	–	–	–	–	–	13	15	19	32	14	7	1	1	–	–	–	–	–	–	–
Private industry	371	39.5	1,196	1,209	1,081 – 1,289	–	–	–	–	–	–	13	15	19	32	14	7	1	1	–	–	–	–	–	–	–
Computer Systems Analyst Supervisors/Managers																										
Level I	216	39.5	1,080	1,068	1,018 – 1,150	–	–	–	–	–	1	16	46	27	4	5	–	–	–	–	–	–	–	–	–	–
Private industry	186	39.6	1,080	1,060	1,014 – 1,165	–	–	–	–	–	2	18	45	26	5	5	–	–	–	–	–	–	–	–	–	–
Service producing	159	39.5	1,071	1,060	1,007 – 1,123	–	–	–	–	–	2	19	49	21	4	5	–	–	–	–	–	–	–	–	–	–
State and local government	30	39.1	1,081	–	– – –	–	–	–	–	–	–	7	57	37	–	–	–	–	–	–	–	–	–	–	–	–
Level II	187	38.4	1,258	1,267	1,181 – 1,352	–	–	–	–	–	–	5	9	17	29	27	12	1	–	–	–	–	–	–	–	–
Private industry	185	38.4	1,256	1,267	1,181 – 1,346	–	–	–	–	–	–	5	9	17	30	27	11	1	–	–	–	–	–	–	–	–
Goods producing	62	38.4	1,288	–	– – –	–	–	–	–	–	–	–	13	8	32	32	15	–	–	–	–	–	–	–	–	–
Manufacturing	62	38.4	1,288	–	– – –	–	–	–	–	–	–	–	13	8	32	32	15	–	–	–	–	–	–	–	–	–
Service producing	123	38.4	1,239	1,233	1,178 – 1,336	–	–	–	–	–	–	8	7	22	28	24	10	1	–	–	–	–	–	–	–	–
Personnel Specialists																										
Level I	59	38.9	499	–	– – –	–	58	39	3	–	–	–	–	–	–	–	–	–	–	–	–	–	–	–	–	–
Private industry	54	39.1	494	–	– – –	–	61	37	2	–	–	–	–	–	–	–	–	–	–	–	–	–	–	–	–	–
Level II	673	38.4	566	565	526 – 602	–	8	65	25	1	([3])	–	–	–	–	–	–	–	–	–	–	–	–	–	–	–
Private industry	595	38.6	562	565	526 – 598	–	9	67	23	1	([3])	–	–	–	–	–	–	–	–	–	–	–	–	–	–	–
Goods producing	135	39.3	575	559	538 – 614	–	4	64	30	3	–	–	–	–	–	–	–	–	–	–	–	–	–	–	–	–
Manufacturing	135	39.3	575	559	538 – 614	–	4	64	30	3	–	–	–	–	–	–	–	–	–	–	–	–	–	–	–	–
Service producing	460	38.4	558	565	518 – 578	–	11	68	20	([3])	([3])	–	–	–	–	–	–	–	–	–	–	–	–	–	–	–
State and local government	78	36.4	598	590	544 – 652	–	–	51	46	3	–	–	–	–	–	–	–	–	–	–	–	–	–	–	–	–
Level III	804	38.9	710	702	640 – 772	–	–	13	35	36	12	3	([3])	([3])	–	–	–	–	–	–	–	–	–	–	–	–
Private industry	712	39.0	709	701	634 – 772	–	–	14	34	34	14	3	1	([3])	–	–	–	–	–	–	–	–	–	–	–	–
Goods producing	263	39.3	709	709	605 – 778	–	–	21	26	37	12	3	1	–	–	–	–	–	–	–	–	–	–	–	–	–
Manufacturing	263	39.3	709	709	605 – 778	–	–	21	26	37	12	3	1	–	–	–	–	–	–	–	–	–	–	–	–	–
Service producing	449	38.8	708	701	645 – 753	–	–	10	39	32	15	3	([3])	([3])	–	–	–	–	–	–	–	–	–	–	–	–
Transportation and utilities	30	38.4	731	–	– – –	–	–	17	30	20	17	17	–	–	–	–	–	–	–	–	–	–	–	–	–	–
State and local government	92	38.5	718	755	667 – 775	–	–	4	38	58	–	–	–	–	–	–	–	–	–	–	–	–	–	–	–	–
Level IV	603	38.5	924	938	829 – 985	–	–	–	2	12	28	37	15	6	–	–	–	–	–	–	–	–	–	–	–	–
Private industry	538	38.5	914	925	826 – 970	–	–	–	2	13	30	37	14	4	–	–	–	–	–	–	–	–	–	–	–	–
Goods producing	193	39.3	970	970	938 – 1,017	–	–	–	–	5	11	56	19	8	–	–	–	–	–	–	–	–	–	–	–	–
Manufacturing	193	39.3	970	970	938 – 1,017	–	–	–	–	5	11	56	19	8	–	–	–	–	–	–	–	–	–	–	–	–
Service producing	345	38.1	882	864	822 – 960	–	–	–	3	17	40	27	11	2	–	–	–	–	–	–	–	–	–	–	–	–
State and local government	65	38.2	1,011	997	922 – 1,099	–	–	–	2	6	11	32	25	25	–	–	–	–	–	–	–	–	–	–	–	–

See footnotes at end of table.

Table A-3. All establishments: Weekly hours and earnings of clerical occupations, Philadelphia, PA-NJ, November 1992

Occupation and level	Number of workers	Average weekly hours[1] (standard)	Weekly earnings (in dollars)[2]			Percent of workers receiving straight-time weekly earnings (in dollars) of—																				
			Mean	Median	Middle range	Under 225	225 and under 250	250 - 275	275 - 300	300 - 325	325 - 350	350 - 375	375 - 400	400 - 425	425 - 450	450 - 500	500 - 550	550 - 600	600 - 650	650 - 700	700 - 750	750 - 800	800 - 850	850 - 950	950 - 1050	1050 - 1150
Clerks, Accounting																										
Level I	248	37.8	$311	$307	$266 – $336	1	4	21	2	45	10	5	4	4	2	2	–	–	–	–	–	–	–	–	–	–
Private industry	240	37.9	311	307	260 – 330	1	5	22	3	45	9	5	4	5	2	2	–	–	–	–	–	–	–	–	–	–
Service producing	211	37.8	313	307	300 – 330	1	5	16	3	49	10	4	4	3	2	2	–	–	–	–	–	–	–	–	–	–
Level II	5,368	38.9	357	354	320 – 390	–	4	6	7	17	13	17	16	8	5	5	1	1	([3])	([3])	–	–	–	–	–	–
Private industry	5,171	39.0	355	353	320 – 388	–	4	6	7	17	13	17	16	8	5	4	1	1	([3])	([3])	–	–	–	–	–	–
Goods producing	1,485	39.1	377	369	337 – 413	–	4	4	5	5	14	23	17	8	5	11	1	3	([3])	([3])	–	–	–	–	–	–
Manufacturing	1,451	39.1	376	368	337 – 410	–	4	4	5	4	14	23	17	8	4	11	1	3	([3])	([3])	–	–	–	–	–	–
Service producing	3,686	38.9	347	344	312 – 380	–	4	7	7	21	12	15	16	8	5	2	1	([3])	([3])	–	–	–	–	–	–	–
Transportation and utilities	109	38.5	409	390	341 – 462	–	–	2	2	16	8	18	6	10	9	12	6	6	5	–	–	–	–	–	–	–
State and local government	197	37.0	392	389	320 – 455	–	–	1	15	14	7	5	18	1	12	13	14	–	–	–	–	–	–	–	–	–
Level III	1,641	38.6	422	416	374 – 465	–	–	–	2	4	6	15	11	18	12	27	4	([3])	1	1	([3])	1	–	–	–	–
Private industry	1,322	38.6	417	404	365 – 453	–	–	–	2	4	5	17	12	20	12	18	5	([3])	2	1	([3])	1	–	–	–	–
Goods producing	301	39.2	422	414	344 – 464	–	–	–	–	14	11	7	11	10	12	20	7	1	7	–	–	–	–	–	–	–
Manufacturing	301	39.2	422	414	344 – 464	–	–	–	–	14	11	7	11	10	12	20	7	1	7	–	–	–	–	–	–	–
Service producing	1,021	38.4	416	403	369 – 447	–	–	–	3	1	4	20	13	23	12	17	4	([3])	([3])	1	([3])	1	–	–	–	–
Transportation and utilities	68	39.0	523	492	356 – 694	–	–	–	12	9	3	4	–	4	13	15	3	–	1	13	4	18	–	–	–	–
State and local government	319	38.7	444	475	427 – 475	–	–	–	–	1	8	4	4	7	11	64	([3])	–	–	–	–	–	–	–	–	–
Level IV	141	38.5	482	493	442 – 534	–	–	–	–	–	3	7	6	8	7	27	34	7	–	–	–	–	1	–	–	–
Private industry	128	38.8	480	494	422 – 534	–	–	–	–	–	3	8	6	9	8	21	37	7	–	–	–	–	2	–	–	–
Service producing	99	38.9	467	469	412 – 525	–	–	–	–	–	4	10	8	11	10	16	36	2	–	–	–	–	2	–	–	–
Clerks, General																										
Level I	133	38.4	260	260	220 – 288	44	5	11	19	13	5	1	3	–	–	–	–	–	–	–	–	–	–	–	–	–
Private industry	122	38.6	254	226	220 – 288	48	5	10	20	11	5	1	–	–	–	–	–	–	–	–	–	–	–	–	–	–
Service producing	107	38.4	245	220	220 – 283	[4]55	6	11	23	3	1	1	–	–	–	–	–	–	–	–	–	–	–	–	–	–
Level II	2,169	38.3	322	319	280 – 358	1	10	10	18	14	16	16	4	7	3	([3])	1	–	–	–	–	–	–	–	–	–
Private industry	1,537	38.6	311	305	270 – 355	1	14	14	17	16	12	13	5	4	3	([3])	2	–	–	–	–	–	–	–	–	–
Goods producing	211	39.7	362	353	319 – 365	–	–	2	9	20	17	28	3	–	7	–	13	–	–	–	–	–	–	–	–	–
Manufacturing	208	39.7	363	355	319 – 365	–	–	2	8	21	17	29	3	–	7	–	13	–	–	–	–	–	–	–	–	–
Service producing	1,326	38.4	303	294	261 – 339	1	17	16	18	15	11	10	6	4	2	([3])	([3])	–	–	–	–	–	–	–	–	–
State and local government	632	37.5	349	344	317 – 363	–	–	–	21	9	25	25	1	15	3	([3])	–	–	–	–	–	–	–	–	–	–
Level III	2,346	38.3	391	401	342 – 427	–	([3])	3	4	4	15	13	7	26	10	11	4	([3])	([3])	–	–	–	–	–	–	–
Private industry	1,441	38.9	378	364	334 – 415	–	([3])	5	7	6	19	19	6	13	8	11	6	([3])	1	–	–	–	–	–	–	–
Goods producing	282	39.9	435	432	400 – 490	–	–	–	–	([3])	([3])	19	5	24	6	34	7	1	3	–	–	–	–	–	–	–
Manufacturing	129	39.9	446	432	403 – 501	–	–	–	–	1	1	12	12	22	13	14	16	2	7	–	–	–	–	–	–	–
Service producing	1,159	38.6	364	356	326 – 401	–	([3])	7	8	7	24	19	6	11	8	5	5	–	–	–	–	–	–	–	–	–
State and local government	905	37.4	411	416	398 – 430	–	–	–	1	2	9	5	10	47	15	10	1	–	–	–	–	–	–	–	–	–
Level IV	619	38.7	429	432	360 – 505	–	–	1	2	10	6	11	5	12	13	15	15	10	([3])	–	–	–	–	–	–	–
Private industry	572	38.9	427	427	360 – 505	–	–	1	2	11	7	12	5	11	13	12	15	11	1	–	–	–	–	–	–	–
Goods producing	74	39.5	449	–	– – –	–	–	–	–	–	–	–	1	22	57	5	9	4	1	–	–	–	–	–	–	–
Manufacturing	74	39.5	449	–	– – –	–	–	–	–	–	–	–	1	22	57	5	9	4	1	–	–	–	–	–	–	–
Service producing	498	38.8	424	413	353 – 505	–	–	1	3	13	8	13	6	9	6	13	16	12	([3])	–	–	–	–	–	–	–
State and local government	47	36.8	450	453	423 – 463	–	–	–	–	–	–	–	–	28	17	51	4	–	–	–	–	–	–	–	–	–

See footnotes at end of table.

Table A-3. All establishments: Weekly hours and earnings of clerical occupations, Philadelphia, PA-NJ, November 1992 — Continued

Occupation and level	Number of workers	Average weekly hours[1] (standard)	Weekly earnings (in dollars)[2] Mean	Median	Middle range	Percent of workers receiving straight-time weekly earnings (in dollars) of— Under 225	225 and under 250	250 - 275	275 - 300	300 - 325	325 - 350	350 - 375	375 - 400	400 - 425	425 - 450	450 - 500	500 - 550	550 - 600	600 - 650	650 - 700	700 - 750	750 - 800	800 - 850	850 - 950	950 - 1050	1050 - 1150
Clerks, Order																										
Level II	283	38.6	$451	$430	$415 – $487	–	–	–	–	–	–	7	9	29	15	20	3	13	2	1	–	–	–	–	–	–
Private industry	283	38.6	451	430	415 – 487	–	–	–	–	–	–	7	9	29	15	20	3	13	2	1	–	–	–	–	–	–
Goods producing	271	38.7	453	430	418 – 487	–	–	–	–	–	–	8	8	27	16	21	3	14	2	1	–	–	–	–	–	–
Manufacturing	271	38.7	453	430	418 – 487	–	–	–	–	–	–	8	8	27	16	21	3	14	2	1	–	–	–	–	–	–
Key Entry Operators																										
Level I	2,340	39.0	313	300	268 – 345	1	16	19	12	19	14	5	3	7	1	3	2	([3])	([3])	–	–	–	–	–	–	–
Private industry	2,314	39.0	312	300	268 – 342	1	16	19	12	19	14	5	2	7	1	3	2	([3])	([3])	–	–	–	–	–	–	–
Goods producing	212	39.2	365	350	337 – 403	–	–	3	10	9	20	25	4	13	–	14	([3])	1	–	–	–	–	–	–	–	–
Manufacturing	212	39.2	365	350	337 – 403	–	–	3	10	9	20	25	4	13	–	14	([3])	1	–	–	–	–	–	–	–	–
Service producing	2,102	39.0	306	297	265 – 340	1	17	21	12	20	13	3	2	6	1	2	2	([3])	([3])	–	–	–	–	–	–	–
Transportation and utilities	88	39.7	377	321	285 – 458	–	–	–	25	25	1	–	5	9	6	18	6	–	6	–	–	–	–	–	–	–
State and local government	26	36.6	422	–	–	–	–	–	–	–	4	–	19	27	38	12	–	–	–	–	–	–	–	–	–	–
Level II	1,272	38.7	387	385	360 – 411	–	–	([3])	1	5	13	27	15	21	7	9	1	–	–	([3])	–	–	–	–	–	–
Private industry	1,223	38.7	385	378	360 – 407	–	–	([3])	1	5	14	28	16	21	5	9	1	–	–	([3])	–	–	–	–	–	–
Goods producing	205	39.3	418	403	366 – 460	–	–	–	–	–	2	24	4	23	14	29	3	–	–	–	–	–	–	–	–	–
Manufacturing	205	39.3	418	403	366 – 460	–	–	–	–	–	2	24	4	23	14	29	3	–	–	–	–	–	–	–	–	–
Service producing	1,018	38.6	378	372	353 – 402	–	–	([3])	2	6	16	29	18	21	4	5	–	–	–	([3])	–	–	–	–	–	–
State and local government	49	36.9	451	444	424 – 464	–	–	–	–	–	–	–	–	27	43	18	12	–	–	–	–	–	–	–	–	–
Personnel Assistants (Employment)																										
Level II	62	37.7	428	–	–	–	–	–	–	–	8	5	23	10	3	45	5	2	–	–	–	–	–	–	–	–
State and local government	37	37.2	441	–	–	–	–	–	–	–	–	3	14	3	5	76	–	–	–	–	–	–	–	–	–	–
Level III	150	38.8	484	480	442 – 528	–	–	–	–	–	–	–	11	10	15	31	15	9	9	1	–	–	–	–	–	–
Private industry	134	39.2	478	461	430 – 519	–	–	–	–	–	–	–	12	11	16	34	10	9	7	1	–	–	–	–	–	–
Goods producing	56	39.8	492	–	–	–	–	–	–	–	–	–	27	9	4	16	11	18	14	2	–	–	–	–	–	–
Manufacturing	56	39.8	492	–	–	–	–	–	–	–	–	–	27	9	4	16	11	18	14	2	–	–	–	–	–	–
Service producing	78	38.7	468	–	–	–	–	–	–	–	–	–	1	13	24	46	10	3	3	–	–	–	–	–	–	–
Secretaries																										
Level I	1,133	38.1	395	388	360 – 420	–	–	([3])	3	5	8	21	23	17	8	10	3	2	1	([3])	–	–	–	–	–	–
Private industry	990	38.3	399	392	365 – 429	–	–	([3])	3	5	8	16	24	17	9	11	3	2	1	([3])	–	–	–	–	–	–
Goods producing	277	39.5	429	442	365 – 461	–	–	–	–	12	5	12	12	5	11	30	6	5	2	([3])	–	–	–	–	–	–
Manufacturing	277	39.5	429	442	365 – 461	–	–	–	–	12	5	12	12	5	11	30	6	5	2	([3])	–	–	–	–	–	–
Service producing	713	37.8	387	388	365 – 405	–	–	([3])	5	3	9	17	29	22	8	4	2	1	([3])	–	–	–	–	–	–	–
State and local government	143	36.6	368	361	357 – 386	–	–	1	1	2	8	57	17	10	3	–	1	–	–	–	–	–	–	–	–	–
Level II	2,859	38.1	428	422	379 – 468	–	–	1	([3])	1	7	14	11	17	15	18	11	4	1	([3])	([3])	–	–	–	–	–
Private industry	2,245	38.4	433	425	385 – 479	–	–	–	([3])	1	6	12	13	17	14	18	13	4	([3])	([3])	([3])	–	–	–	–	–
Goods producing	537	39.4	438	428	396 – 506	–	–	–	([3])	3	6	9	9	21	8	15	26	2	–	–	–	–	–	–	–	–
Manufacturing	537	39.4	438	428	396 – 506	–	–	–	([3])	3	6	9	9	21	8	15	26	2	–	–	–	–	–	–	–	–
Service producing	1,708	38.0	431	425	384 – 468	–	–	–	([3])	1	6	13	14	15	16	19	9	5	([3])	([3])	([3])	–	–	–	–	–
State and local government	614	37.3	410	413	366 – 442	–	–	4	2	2	9	21	5	18	15	15	4	4	1	–	–	–	–	–	–	–

See footnotes at end of table.

Table A-3. All establishments: Weekly hours and earnings of clerical occupations, Philadelphia, PA-NJ, November 1992 — Continued

Occupation and level	Number of workers	Average weekly hours[1] (standard)	Weekly earnings (in dollars)[2]			Percent of workers receiving straight-time weekly earnings (in dollars) of—																				
			Mean	Median	Middle range	Under 225	225 and under 250	250 - 275	275 - 300	300 - 325	325 - 350	350 - 375	375 - 400	400 - 425	425 - 450	450 - 500	500 - 550	550 - 600	600 - 650	650 - 700	700 - 750	750 - 800	800 - 850	850 - 950	950 - 1050	1050 - 1150
Level III	5,606	38.6	$494	$486	$447 – $528	–	–	(3)	(3)	(3)	1	3	3	9	11	32	23	9	5	1	1	(3)	(3)	1	–	–
Private industry	4,714	38.7	498	490	448 – 530	–	–	(3)	(3)	(3)	1	2	4	9	10	32	25	10	4	1	1	(3)	(3)	1	–	–
Goods producing	1,662	39.4	517	506	473 – 553	–	–	–	–	–	–	(3)	(3)	4	8	33	29	15	6	2	2	(3)	(3)	–	–	–
Manufacturing	1,624	39.4	517	504	471 – 554	–	–	–	–	–	–	(3)	(3)	4	9	33	27	16	6	2	2	(3)	(3)	–	–	–
Service producing	3,052	38.3	488	483	433 – 520	–	–	(3)	(3)	(3)	1	4	5	11	11	31	23	7	3	1	(3)	1	(3)	2	–	–
Transportation and utilities	186	39.4	669	657	516 – 899	–	–	–	–	–	–	6	–	4	3	7	9	13	6	12	2	7	1	29	–	–
State and local government	892	37.9	473	461	436 – 506	–	–	–	–	1	1	6	2	12	15	35	11	9	8	(3)	–	–	–	–	–	–
Level IV	2,087	38.5	564	562	516 – 609	–	–	–	–	–	(3)	1	2	2	3	12	24	28	15	8	2	2	(3)	(3)	(3)	–
Private industry	1,845	38.5	565	564	515 – 609	–	–	–	–	–	(3)	1	2	2	3	12	21	30	16	8	2	2	(3)	(3)	(3)	–
Goods producing	613	38.2	593	586	547 – 633	–	–	–	–	–	–	–	–	–	–	5	22	38	17	13	2	3	(3)	(3)	–	–
Manufacturing	613	38.2	593	586	547 – 633	–	–	–	–	–	–	–	–	–	–	5	22	38	17	13	2	3	(3)	(3)	–	–
Service producing	1,232	38.6	551	552	497 – 597	–	–	–	–	–	(3)	2	3	3	4	16	21	27	15	5	2	1	(3)	1	(3)	–
Transportation and utilities	89	39.0	683	666	597 – 743	–	–	–	–	–	–	–	–	–	–	3	7	16	17	20	12	12	–	7	6	–
State and local government	242	38.2	561	528	528 – 612	–	–	–	–	–	–	4	–	–	–	10	48	9	13	13	4	–	–	–	–	–
Level V	384	39.5	663	641	593 – 714	–	–	–	–	–	–	–	–	–	1	5	8	17	20	18	15	6	2	3	2	3
Private industry	383	39.5	664	641	593 – 714	–	–	–	–	–	–	–	–	–	1	5	8	17	20	18	15	6	2	3	2	3
Goods producing	224	39.8	623	603	565 – 680	–	–	–	–	–	–	–	–	–	1	8	10	26	19	19	8	4	1	3	–	–
Manufacturing	224	39.8	623	603	565 – 680	–	–	–	–	–	–	–	–	–	1	8	10	26	19	19	8	4	1	3	–	–
Service producing	159	39.0	721	703	618 – 774	–	–	–	–	–	–	–	–	–	–	1	6	4	21	17	23	8	3	3	5	8
Switchboard Operator-Receptionists	2,205	38.6	342	344	303 – 380	6	3	5	8	17	17	15	16	4	3	4	2	(3)	–	–	(3)	–	–	–	–	–
Private industry	2,078	38.7	339	340	300 – 375	7	3	5	9	16	18	15	15	4	2	3	3	(3)	–	–	(3)	–	–	–	–	–
Goods producing	705	39.5	357	350	325 – 370	–	2	–	4	18	23	32	10	2	(3)	7	3	(3)	–	–	–	–	–	–	–	–
Manufacturing	694	39.4	357	350	325 – 370	–	2	–	4	18	21	32	10	2	(3)	7	3	(3)	–	–	–	–	–	–	–	–
Service producing	1,373	38.3	330	339	282 – 379	10	3	7	11	16	16	7	17	5	3	2	2	1	–	–	(3)	–	–	–	–	–
Transportation and utilities	56	39.1	337	291	280 – 340	–	–	–	61	13	14	4	–	–	–	–	–	–	–	–	9	–	–	–	–	–
State and local government	127	37.5	389	395	367 – 428	–	–	2	–	19	2	9	30	5	21	13	–	–	–	–	–	–	–	–	–	–
Word Processors																										
Level I	234	38.4	370	360	329 – 409	–	1	1	17	5	13	22	13	8	11	5	3	1	1	–	–	–	–	–	–	–
Private industry	229	38.5	370	360	328 – 409	–	1	1	17	5	13	23	12	7	11	5	3	1	1	–	–	–	–	–	–	–
Service producing	189	38.4	358	354	311 – 385	–	1	2	21	6	15	23	12	8	5	2	3	1	1	–	–	–	–	–	–	–
Level II	546	37.9	417	415	382 – 443	–	–	–	1	1	8	14	15	26	14	14	5	2	1	–	–	–	–	–	–	–
Private industry	371	38.1	426	422	387 – 456	–	–	–	1	2	4	14	12	25	15	18	6	3	1	–	–	–	–	–	–	–
Goods producing	78	37.7	456	–	– – –	–	–	–	–	–	–	1	5	26	24	32	6	5	–	–	–	–	–	–	–	–
Manufacturing	78	37.7	456	–	– – –	–	–	–	–	–	–	1	5	26	24	32	6	5	–	–	–	–	–	–	–	–
Service producing	293	38.2	419	417	374 – 444	–	–	–	1	2	5	17	13	25	13	14	6	2	2	–	–	–	–	–	–	–
State and local government	175	37.5	396	396	354 – 422	–	–	–	1	–	15	15	21	28	12	6	2	–	–	–	–	–	–	–	–	–

[1] Standard hours reflect the workweek for which employees receive their regular straight-time salaries (exclusive of pay for overtime at regular and/or premium rates), and the earnings correspond to these weekly hours.

[2] Excludes premium pay for overtime and for work on weekends, holidays, and late shifts. Also excluded are performance bonuses and lump-sum payments of the type negotiated in the auto and aerospace industries, as well as profit-sharing payments, attendance bonuses, Christmas or year-end bonuses, and other nonproduction bonuses. Pay increases, but not bonuses, under cost-of-living clauses, and incentive payments, however, are included. See Appendix A for definitions and methods used to compute means, medians, and middle ranges.

[3] Less than 0.5 percent.

[4] All workers were at $200 and under $225.

NOTE: Because of rounding, sums of individual intervals may not equal 100 percent. Dashes indicate that no data were reported or that data did not meet publication criteria. Overall occupation or occupational levels may include data for categories not shown separately.

Personnel Assistant (Employment) IV

Performs work in support of personnel professionals which requires a good working knowledge of personnel procedures, guides, and precedents. In representative assignments: interviews applicants, obtains references, and recommends placement of applicants in a few well-defined occupations (trades or clerical) within a stable organization or unit; conducts post-placement or exit interviews to identify job adjustment problems or reasons for leaving the organization; performs routine statistical analyses related to manpower, EEO, hiring, or other employment concerns, e.g., compares one set of data to another set as instructed; and requisitions applicants through employment agencies for clerical or blue-collar jobs. At this level, assistants typically have a range of personal contacts within and outside the organization and with applicants, and must be tactful and articulate. May perform some clerical work in addition to the above duties. Supervisor reviews completed work against stated objectives.

SECRETARY

(4622: Secretary)

Provides principal secretarial support in an office, usually to one individual, and, in some cases, also to the subordinate staff of that individual. Maintains a close and highly responsive relationship to the day-to-day activities of the supervisor and staff. Works fairly independently receiving a minimum of detailed supervision and guidance. Performs varied clerical and secretarial duties requiring a knowledge of office routine and an understanding of the organization, programs, and procedures related to the work of the office.

Exclusions. Not all positions titled "secretary" possess the above characteristics. Examples of positions which are excluded from the definition are as follows:

a. Clerks or secretaries working under the direction of secretaries or administrative assistants as described in e;

b. Stenographers not fully performing secretarial duties;

c. Stenographers or secretaries assigned to two or more professional, technical, or managerial persons of equivalent rank;

d. Assistants or secretaries performing any kind of technical work, e.g., personnel, accounting, or legal work;

e. Administrative assistants or supervisors performing duties which are more difficult or more responsible than the secretarial work described in LR-1 through LR-4;

f. Secretaries receiving additional pay primarily for maintaining confidentiality of payroll records or other sensitive information;

g. Secretaries performing routine receptionist, typing, and filing duties following detailed instructions and guidelines; these duties are less responsible than those described in LR-1 below; and

h. Trainees.

Classification by level

Secretary jobs which meet the required characteristics are matched at one of five levels according to two factors: (a) level of the secretary's supervisor within the overall organizational structure, and (b) level of the secretary's responsibility. The table following the explanations of these factors indicates the level of the secretary for each combination of factors.

Level of secretary's supervisor (LS)

Secretaries should be matched at one of the three LS levels below best describing the organization of the secretary's supervisor.

LS-1 Organizational structure is not complex and internal procedures and administrative controls are simple and informal; supervisor directs staff through face-to-face meetings.

LS-2 Organizational structure is complex and is divided into *subordinate groups that usually differ from each other as to subject-matter, function, etc.*; supervisor usually directs staff through intermediate supervisors; and internal procedures and administrative controls are formal. An entire organization (e.g., division, subsidiary, or parent organization) may contain a variety of subordinate groups which meet the LS-2 definition. Therefore, it is not unusual for one LS-2 supervisor to report to another LS-2 supervisor.

The presence of subordinate supervisors does not by itself mean LS-2 applies, e.g., a clerical processing organization divided into several units, each performing very similar work is placed in LS-1.

In smaller organizations or industries such as retail trade, with relatively few organizational levels, the supervisor may have an impact on the policies and major programs of the entire organization, and may deal with important outside contacts, as described in LS-3.

LS-3 Organizational structure is divided into two or more subordinate supervisory levels (of which at least one is a managerial level) with several subdivisions at each level. Executive's program(s) are usually inter-locked on a direct and continuing basis with other major organizational segments, requiring constant attention to extensive formal coordination, clearances, and procedural controls. Executive typically has: financial decision making authority for assigned program(s); considerable impact on the entire organization's financial position or public image; and responsibility for, or has staff specialists in, such areas as personnel and administration for assigned organization. Executive plays an important role in determining the policies and major programs of the entire organization, and spends considerable time dealing with outside parties actively interested in assigned program(s) and current or controversial issues.

Level of secretary's responsibility (LR)

This factor evaluates the nature of the work relationship between the secretary and the supervisor or staff, and the extent to which the secretary is expected to exercise initiative and judgment. Secretaries should be matched at the level best describing their level of responsibility. When the position's duties span more than one LR level, the introductory paragraph at the beginning of each LR level should be used to determine which of the levels best matches the position. (Typically, secretaries performing at the higher levels of responsibility also perform duties described at the lower levels.)

LR-1 Carries out *recurring* office procedures independently. Selects the guideline or reference which fits the specific case. Supervisor provides specific instructions on new assignments and checks completed work for accuracy. Performs varied duties including or comparable to the following:

a. Responds to routine telephone requests which have standard answers; refers calls and visitors to appropriate staff. Controls mail and assures timely staff response; may send form letters.

b. As instructed, maintains supervisor's calendar, makes appointments, and arranges for meeting rooms.

c. Reviews materials prepared for supervisor's approval for typographical accuracy and proper format.

d. Maintains recurring internal reports, such as: time and leave records, office equipment listings, correspondence controls, training plans, etc.

e. Requisitions supplies, printing, maintenance, or other services. Types, takes and transcribes dictation, and establishes and maintains office files.

LR-2 Handles differing situations, problems, and deviations in the work of the office according to the supervisor's general instructions, priorities, duties, policies, and program goals. Supervisor may assist secretary with special assignments. Duties include or are comparable to the following:

a. Screens telephone calls, visitors, and incoming correspondence; personally responds to requests for information concerning office procedures; determines which requests should be handled by the supervisor, appropriate staff member, or other offices. May prepare and sign routine, non-technical correspondence in own or supervisor's name.

b. Schedules tentative appointments without prior clearance. Makes arrangements for conferences and meetings and assembles established background materials, as directed. May attend meetings and record and report on the proceedings.

c. Reviews outgoing materials and correspondence for internal consistency and conformance with supervisor's procedures; assures that proper clearances have been obtained, when needed.

d. Collects information from the files or staff for routine inquires on office program(s) or periodic reports. Refers nonroutine requests to supervisor or staff.

e. Explains to subordinate staff supervisor's requirements concerning office procedures. Coordinates personnel and administrative forms for the office and forwards for processing.

LR-3 Uses greater judgment and initiative to determine the approach or action to take in nonroutine situations. Interprets and adapts guidelines, including unwritten policies, precedents, and practices, which are not always completely applicable to changing situations. Duties include or are comparable to the following:

a. Based on a knowledge of the supervisor's views, composes correspondence on own initiative about administrative matters and general office policies for supervisor's approval.

b. Anticipates and prepares materials needed by the supervisor for conferences, correspondence, appointments, meetings, telephone calls, etc., and informs supervisor on matters to be considered.

c. Reads publications, regulations, and directives and takes action or refers those that are important to the supervisor and staff.

d. Prepares special or one-time reports, summaries, or replies to inquires, selecting relevant information from a variety of sources such as reports, documents, correspondence, other offices, etc., under general direction.

e. Advises secretaries in subordinate offices on new procedures; requests information needed from the subordinate office(s) for periodic or special conferences, reports, inquires, etc. Shifts clerical staff to accommodate work load needs.

LR-4 Handles a wide variety of situations and conflicts involving the clerical or administrative functions of the office which often cannot be brought to the attention of the executive. The executive sets the overall objectives of the work. Secretary may participate in developing the work deadlines. Duties include or are comparable to the following:

a. Composes correspondence requiring some understanding of technical matters; may sign for executive when technical or policy content has been authorized.

b. Notes commitments made by executive during meetings and arranges for staff implementation. On own initiative, arranges for staff member to represent organization at conferences and meetings, establishes appointment priorities, or reschedules or refuses appointments or invitations.

c. Reads outgoing correspondence for executive's approval and alerts writers to any conflict with the file or departure from policies or executive's viewpoints; gives advice to resolve the problems.

d. Summarizes the content of incoming materials, specially gathered information, or meetings to assist executive; coordinates the new information with background office sources; draws attention to important parts or conflicts.

e. In the executive's absence, ensures that requests for action or information are relayed to the appropriate staff member; as needed, interprets request and helps implement action; makes sure that information is furnished in timely manner; decides whether executive should be notified of important or emergency matters.

Exclude secretaries performing any of the following duties:

a. Acts as office manager for the executive's organization, e.g., determines when new procedures are needed for changing situations and devises and implements alternatives; revises or clarifies procedures to eliminate conflict or duplication; identifies and resolves various problems that affect the orderly flow of work in transactions with parties outside the organization.

b. Prepares agenda for conferences; explains discussion topics to participants; drafts introductions and develops background information and prepares outlines for executive or staff member(s) to use in writing speeches.

c. Advises individuals outside the organization on the executive's views on major policies or current issues facing the organization; contacts or responds to contacts from high-ranking outside officials (e.g., city or State officials, Member of Congress, presidents of national unions or large national or international firms, etc.) in unique situations. These officials may be relatively inaccessible, and each contact typically must be handled differently, using judgment and discretion.

Criteria for matching secretaries by level

Level of secretary's supervisor	Level of secretary's responsibility LR-1	LR-2	LR-3	LR-4
LS-1	I*	II	III	IV
LS-2	I*	III	IV	V
LS-3	I*	IV	V	V

*Regardless of LS level.

SWITCHBOARD OPERATOR-RECEPTIONIST
(4645: Receptionist)

Operates a single-position telephone switchboard or console, used with a private branch exchange (PBX) system to relay incoming, outgoing, and intrasystem calls *and* acts as a receptionist greeting visitors, determining nature of visits and directing visitors to appropriate persons. Work may also involve other duties such as recording and transmitting messages; keeping records of calls placed; providing information to callers and visitors; making appointments; keeping a log of visitors; and issuing visitor passes. May also type and perform other routine clerical work, usually while at the switchboard or console, which may occupy the major portion of the worker's time.

WORD PROCESSOR
(4624: Typist)

Uses automated systems, such as word processing equipment, or personal computers or work stations linked to a larger computer or local area network, to produce a variety of documents, such as correspondence, memos, publications, forms, reports, tables and graphs. Uses one or more word processing software packages. May also perform routine clerical tasks, such as operating copiers, filing, answering telephones, and sorting and distributing mail.

Excluded are:

a. Typists using automatic or manual typewriters with limited or no text-editing capabilities; workers in these positions are not typically required to use word processing software packages;

SALARY DISTRIBUTIONS IN THE UNITED STATES

(in thousands of U.S. dollars) (<$15,000-$100,000 in $5,000 increments; >$100,000 in $10,000 increments)

Benchmark Job Titles	Positions in the U.S. (in thousands of U.S. dollars)																										
	<15	15-19	20-24	25-29	30-34	35-39	40-44	45-49	50-54	55-59	60-64	65-69	70-74	75-79	80-84	85-89	90-94	95-99	100-109	110-119	120-129	130-139	140-149	150-159	160-169	170-179	180-189	200 >
Principal Administrator			6	16	51	86	80	83	93	70	73	52	52	43	44	18	38	25	38	33	27	24	13	18	11	6	6	15
Administrative/Office Mgr.	1	2	9	35	53	72	59	67	44	37	26	12	6	10	7	2	1		1	2	3	1						1
Comptroller/Finance Dir.			2	8	19	25	29	25	35	24	33	17	21	18	23	9	9	8	9	7	7	3			1	1		
Branch Office Manager		1	5	26	40	42	55	38	28	23	18	14	10	13	7	6	4	3	4	2			1	1				
Accounting Manager		6	8	41	53	55	66	57	27	16	15	3	4	4	4	3			1									
Accounting Supervisor		4	18	38	55	56	41	21	11	8	2	2	2															
Information Services Mgr.		1	2	9	15	32	28	33	25	18	15	15	14	8	8	8	3	3	5	4	1	1						
Librarian	7	17	36	44	64	47	64	33	38	18	15	7	3	5		4	1	2	1									
Legal Assistant Manager			1	2	16	16	19	21	16	17	12	4	4	3	2			1										
Computer Systems Manager		2	10	30	30	27	39	18	18	8	10	4	1	2			3	2	2									
Network Administrator		4	18	27	42	47	47	24	11	5	4		1		2	2												
Marketing Administrator	2		10	11	19	16	28	21	20	16	5	9	6	6	3	2	5	2	4				1					
Office Services Manager	2	22	30	46	56	45	34	24	18	17	10	6	5	1	3	1	1											
Personnel Manager	1	2	4	9	33	45	39	57	26	32	19	10	9	8	5		1	1	3									
Recruitment Administrator	1	1	5	9	28	24	31	21	10	10	9	8	2		1		2		1									
Document Production Mgr.		3	1	5	13	17	16	8	7	2	3	1	1			1												
Records Manager	3	35	38	40	38	42	24	14	15	4		2	1	1														

Source: Association of Legal Administrators

Compensation of Office Services Managers
in the U.S. (in U.S. dollars)

Variable & Category	No. in Job	Mean	First Decile	First Quartile	Median	Third Quartile	Ninth Decile
All Such Respondents							
Base Annual Salary	321	$38,044	$21,480	$28,000	$35,500	$46,125	$58,096
Total Annual Cash Compensation	321	$40,135	$21,726	$29,210	$36,900	$48,625	$63,880
By Region							
Northeastern States (CT, MA, ME, NH, NJ, NY, PA, RI, VT)							
Base Annual Salary	87	$44,854	$29,135	$33,000	$41,039	$55,875	$68,240
Total Annual Cash Compensation	87	$47,473	$29,452	$34,286	$44,000	$60,101	$74,098
Southern States (AL, DC, DE, FL, GA, KY, MD, MS, NC, PR, SC, TN, VA, WV)							
Base Annual Salary	65	$34,811	$18,400	$23,187	$34,485	$42,550	$51,850
Total Annual Cash Compensation	65	$36,645	$20,000	$23,512	$35,450	$44,875	$55,700
Midwestern States (IL, IN, MI, OH, WI)							
Base Annual Salary	42	$38,298	$22,745	$29,300	$35,600	$43,500	$57,450
Total Annual Cash Compensation	42	$40,469	$23,004	$29,661	$36,700	$44,200	$66,070
North Central States (IA, KS, MN, MO, ND, NE, SD)							
Base Annual Salary	13	$31,768	- - - -	$29,000	$32,000	$35,287	- - - -
Total Annual Cash Compensation	13	$32,502	- - - -	$29,025	$32,000	$38,069	- - - -
Southwestern States (AR, LA, OK, TX)							
Base Annual Salary	38	$35,050	$19,240	$25,000	$30,314	$44,400	$59,340
Total Annual Cash Compensation	38	$37,955	$20,095	$25,216	$33,585	$47,980	$69,175
Mountain States (AZ, CO, ID, MT, NM, NV, UT, WY)							
Base Annual Salary	12	$31,922	- - - -	$22,500	$29,065	$38,304	- - - -
Total Annual Cash Compensation	12	$33,232	- - - -	$22,887	$32,015	$41,987	- - - -
Pacific States (AK, CA, GU, HI, OR, WA)							
Base Annual Salary	64	$36,102	$24,600	$28,800	$34,000	$42,650	$52,628
Total Annual Cash Compensation	64	$37,626	$24,663	$29,490	$34,827	$45,732	$53,802
By State							
California							
Base Annual Salary	49	$38,139	$27,048	$29,795	$36,401	$44,722	$54,108
Total Annual Cash Compensation	49	$39,562	$27,472	$30,675	$36,401	$47,100	$55,437
Connecticut							
Base Annual Salary	8	$38,930	- - - -	- - - -	$34,750	- - - -	- - - -
Total Annual Cash Compensation	8	$40,617	- - - -	- - - -	$36,450	- - - -	- - - -
District of Columbia							
Base Annual Salary	17	$44,806	- - - -	$36,425	$40,500	$47,600	- - - -
Total Annual Cash Compensation	17	$47,085	- - - -	$36,625	$44,109	$51,065	- - - -
Florida							
Base Annual Salary	18	$26,147	- - - -	$19,000	$25,415	$31,356	- - - -
Total Annual Cash Compensation	18	$27,716	- - - -	$21,000	$26,325	$32,006	- - - -
Georgia							
Base Annual Salary	5	$53,400	- - - -	- - - -	$57,500	- - - -	- - - -
Total Annual Cash Compensation	5	$56,546	- - - -	- - - -	$57,500	- - - -	- - - -
Illinois							
Base Annual Salary	16	$44,658	- - - -	$36,250	$41,510	$54,450	- - - -
Total Annual Cash Compensation	16	$48,043	- - - -	$36,387	$44,000	$61,763	- - - -

Source: Association of Legal Administrators

Index

Selected Books From... THE SECTION OF LAW PRACTICE MANAGEMENT

ABA Guide to International Business Negotiations. A guide to the general, legal, and cultural issues that arise during international negotiations.

ABA Guide to Legal Marketing. A collection of new and innovative marketing ideas and strategies for lawyers and firms.

ACCESS 1994. An updated guidebook to technology resources. Includes practical hints, practical tips, commonly used terms, and resource information.

Becoming Computer Literate. A guide to computer basics for lawyers and other legal professionals.

Beyond the Billable Hour. A collection of 26 articles discussing issues related to alternative billing methods.

Breaking Traditions. A guide to progressive, flexible, and sensible work alternatives for lawyers who want to balance the demand of the legal profession with other commitments. Model policy for childbirth and parenting leave is included.

Changing Jobs, 2nd Ed. A handbook designed to help lawyers make changes in their professional careers. Includes career planning advice from nearly 50 experts.

Flying Solo: A Survival Guide for the Solo Lawyer, 2nd Ed. An updated and expanded guide to the problems and issues unique to the solo practitioner.

How to Draft Bills Clients Rush to Pay. A collection of techniques for drafting bills that project honesty, competence, fairness and value and how draft an inviting statement.

How to Start and Build a Law Practice, 3rd Ed. Jay Foonberg's classic guide has been updated and expanded. Included are more than 10 new chapters on marketing, financing, automation, practicing from home, ethics and professional responsibility.

Last Frontier: Women Lawyers as Rainmakers. Explains why rainmaking is different for women than men and focuses on ways to improve these skills. Shares the experiences of four women who have successfully built their own practices.

Lawyer's Guide to the Internet. A no-nonsense guide to what the Internet is (and isn't), how it applies to the legal profession, and the different ways it can -- and should -- be used.

Leveraging with Legal Assistants. Reviews the changes that have led to increased use of legal assistants and the need to enlarge their role further. Learn specific ways in which a legal assistant can handle a substantial portion of traditional lawyer work.

Making Partner: A Guide for Law Firm Associates. Written by a managing partner, this book offers guidelines and recommendations designed to help you increase your chances of making partner.

Planning the Small Law Office Library. A step-by-step guide to planning, building, and managing a small law office library. Includes case studies, floor plans, and questionnaires.

Practical Systems: Tips for Organizing Your Law Office.
It will help you get control of your in-box by outlining systems for managing daily work.

Results-Oriented Financial Management: A Guide to Successful Law Firm Financial Performance. How to manage "the numbers," from setting rates and computing billable hours to calculating net income and preparing the budget. Over 30 charts and statements to help you prepare reports.

Survival Skills for the Practicing Lawyer. Includes 29 articles from *Law Practice Management* magazine for the attorney with little or no management responsibilities.

Through the Client's Eyes: New Approaches to Get Clients to Hire You Again and Again. Includes an overview of client relations and sample letters, surveys, and self-assessment questions to gauge your client relations acumen.

Win-Win Billing Strategies. Represents the first comprehensive analysis of what constitutes "value," and how to bill for it. You'll learn how to initiate and implement different billing methods that make sense for you and your client.

TQM in Action: One Firm's Journey Toward Quality and Excellence. A guide to implementing the principles of Total Quality Management in your law firm.

Winning with Computers, Part 1. Addresses virtually every aspect of the use of computers in litigation. You'll get an overview of products available and tips on how to put them to good use. For the beginning and advanced computer user.

Winning with Computers, Part 2. Expands on the ways you can use computers to manage the routine and not-so-routine aspects of your trial practice. Learn how to apply general purpose software and even how to have fun with your computer.

Women Rainmakers' 101+ Best Marketing Tips. A collection of over 130 marketing tips suggested by women rainmakers throughout the country. Includes tips on image, networking, public relations, and advertising.

WordPerfect® in One Hour for Lawyers. This is a crash course in the most popular word processing software package used by lawyers. In four easy lessons, you'll learn the basic steps for getting a simple job done.

WordPerfect® Shortcuts for Lawyers: Learning Merge and Macros in One Hour. A fast-track guide to two of WordPerfect's more advanced functions: merge and macros. Includes 4 lessons designed to take 15 minutes each.

Your New Lawyer, 2nd Ed. A complete legal employer's guide to recruitment, development, and management of new lawyers. Updated to address the many changes in the practice of law since the 1983 edition.

Order Form

Qty	Title	LPM Price	Regular Price	Total
______	ABA Guide to Int'l Business Negotiations (511-0331)	$ 74.95	$ 84.95	$________
______	ABA Guide to Legal Marketing (511-0341)	69.95	79.95	$________
______	ACCESS 1994 (511-0327)	29.95	34.95	$________
______	Becoming Computer Literate (511-0342)	32.95	39.95	$________
______	Beyond the Billable Hour (511-0260)	69.95	79.95	$________
______	Breaking Traditions (511-0320)	64.95	74.95	$________
______	Changing Jobs, 2nd Ed. (511-0334)	49.95	59.95	$________
______	Flying Solo, 2nd Ed. (511-0328)	59.95	69.95	$________
______	How to Draft Bills Clients Rush to Pay (511-0344)	39.95	49.95	$________
______	How to Start & Build a Law Practice, 3rd Ed. (511-0293)	32.95	39.95	$________
______	Last Frontier (511-0314)	9.95	14.95	$________
______	Lawyer's Guide to the Internet (511-0343)	24.95	29.95	$________
______	Leveraging with Legal Assistants (511-0322)	59.95	69.95	$________
______	Making Partner (511-0303)	14.95	19.95	$________
______	Planning the Small Law Office Library (511-0325)	29.95	39.95	$________
______	Practical Systems (511-0296)	24.95	34.95	$________
______	Results-Oriented Financial Management (511-0319)	44.95	54.95	$________
______	Survival Skills for the Practicing Lawyer (511-0324)	39.95	49.95	$________
______	Through the Client's Eyes (511-0337)	69.95	79.95	$________
______	TQM in Action (511-0323)	59.95	69.95	$________
______	Win-Win Billing Strategies (511-0304)	89.95	99.95	$________
______	Winning with Computers, Part 1 (511-0294)	89.95	99.95	$________
______	Winning with Computers, Part 2 (511-0315)	59.95	69.95	$________
______	Winning with Computers, Parts 1 & 2 (511-0316)	124.90	144.90	$________
______	Women Rainmakers' 101+ Best Marketing Tips (511-0336)	14.95	19.95	$________
______	WordPerfect® in One Hour for Lawyers (511-0308)	9.95	14.95	$________
______	WordPerfect® Shortcuts for Lawyers (511-0329)	14.95	19.95	$________
______	Your New Lawyer, 2nd Ed. (511-0312)	74.95	84.95	$________

*HANDLING

$ 2.00-$9.99	$2.00
10.00-24.99	$3.95
25.00-49.99	$4.95
50.00 + ...	$5.95

**TAX

DC residents add 5.75%
IL residents add 8.75%
MD residents add 5%

SUBTOTAL: $________
*HANDLING: $________
**TAX: $________

TOTAL: $________

PAYMENT

☐ Check enclosed (Payable to the ABA) ☐ Bill Me

☐ Visa ☐ MasterCard Account Number:__________-__________-__________-__________

Exp. Date: __________ Signature ______________________________

Name____

Firm____

Address____

City______________________State______________ZIP______________

Phone number______________________________

Mail to: ABA, Publication Orders, P.O. Box 10892, Chicago, IL 60610-0892

PHONE: (312) 988-5522
Or FAX: (312) 988-5568

BOOK

CUSTOMER COMMENT FORM

Title of Book:____________________________________

We've tried to make this publication as useful, accurate, and readable as possible. Please take 5 minutes to tell us if we succeeded. Your comments and suggestions will help us improve our publications. Thank you!

1. How did you acquire this publication:

☐ by mail order ☐ at a meeting/convention ☐ as a gift

☐ by phone order ☐ at a bookstore ☐ don't know

☐ other: (describe) ____________________________________

Please rate this publication as follows:

	Excellent	Good	Fair	Poor	Not Applicable
Readability: Was the book easy to read and understand?	☐	☐	☐	☐	☐
Examples/Cases: Were they helpful, practical? Were there enough?	☐	☐	☐	☐	☐
Content: Did the book meet your expectations? Did it cover the subject adequately?	☐	☐	☐	☐	☐
Organization and clarity: Was the sequence of text logical? Was it easy to find what you wanted to know?	☐	☐	☐	☐	☐
Illustrations/forms/checklists: Were they clear and useful? Were there enough?	☐	☐	☐	☐	☐
Physical attractiveness: What did you think of the appearance of the publication (typesetting, printing, etc.)?	☐	☐	☐	☐	☐

Would you recommend this book to another attorney/administrator? ☐ Yes ☐ No

How could this publication be improved? What else would you like to see in it?

____

Do you have other comments or suggestions? ____________________

Name ____________________

Firm/Company ____________________

Address ____________________

City/State/Zip ____________________

Phone ____________________

Firm Size: __________ Area of specialization: __________

We appreciate your time and help.

Fold

NO POSTAGE
NECESSARY
IF MAILED
IN THE
UNITED STATES

BUSINESS REPLY MAIL

FIRST CLASS PERMIT NO. 16471 CHICAGO, ILLINOIS

POSTAGE WILL BE PAID BY ADDRESSEE

AMERICAN BAR ASSOCIATION
PPM, 8th FLOOR
750 N. LAKE SHORE DRIVE
CHICAGO, ILLINOIS 60611-9851

Fold